Women in Muslim Family Law

Contemporary Issues in the Middle East

Other titles in Contemporary Issues in the Middle East

Women in Muslim Family Law

SECOND EDITION

John L. Esposito

with Natana J. DeLong-Bas

Syracuse University Press

Library of Congress Cataloging-in-Publication Data

Esposito, John L.
    Women in Muslim family law / John L. Esposito with Natana J. DeLong-Bas.—2nd ed.
        p. cm.
    Includes bibliographical references and index.
    ISBN 0-8156-2908-7 (pbk.)
        1. Women—Legal status, laws, etc. (Islamic law) 2. Domestic relations (Islamic law) I.
    DeLong-Bas, Natana J. II. Title.
    LAW
    346.5601'34—dc21   2001034382

Manufactured in the United States of America

For Jean and my parents,
who are always there.

John L. Esposito is University Professor at Georgetown University and director of the Center for Muslim-Christian Understanding in the Edmund A. Walsh School of Foreign Service. He is also the editor-in-chief of *The Oxford Encyclopedia of the Modern Islamic World* and *The Oxford History of Islam*. His other publications include *Islam and Politics, The Islamic Threat: Myth or Reality? Islam and Democracy and Makers of Contemporary Islam* (with John O. Voll); *Islam: The Straight Path;* and *Islam, Gender and Social Change* (with Yvonne Haddad).

Natana J. DeLong-Bas is a Ph.D. candidate in history at Georgetown University. She is completing her dissertation on Islamic law, women and gender, and religious violence in the works of Muhammad Ibn Abd al-Wahhab and is a contributor to and editor for the forthcoming *Oxford Dictionary of Islam*.

Contents

Preface

MUCH HAS OCCURRED in the world of Islam since the publication of the first edition of *Women in Muslim Family Law*. Islam has continued to play a significant role in the political and social development of Muslim societies. New Islamic republics and Muslim governments have been established. Islamic activism has found expression not only in radical politics but also in mainstream politics and society. Islamic organizations and candidates have participated successfully in electoral politics, demonstrating the extent to which in many countries they constitute the only viable opposition or alternative. Islamists have been elected mayors and parliamentarians and have served in cabinets and as prime minister of Turkey and deputy prime minister of Malaysia.

At the same time, Islam has proven an effective social force; Islamically inspired schools, clinics, social welfare services, and insurance and finance companies have proliferated. Governments faced with crises of identity and political legitimacy, whatever their orientation, have witnessed the Islamization of rhetoric and society, accompanied by pressures to reformulate ideas, values, and legislation within an Islamic framework. Unlike "traditionalists," mainstream Islamists are not necessarily against certain legal reforms and women's participation in the political arena, provided that changes are legitimated within an Islamic framework and that women preserve and reflect Islamic identity, conduct, and values. If some call for the implementation of Islamic law *(Shariah)*, others call for the Islamization of existing laws.

Pakistan, Sudan, Iran, and especially Afghanistan, where the Taliban has used heavy-handed enforcement of sexual segregation and veiling, are often cited as examples of the oppressive implementation of *Shariah* by those arguing that international standards of human rights and Islamic law are not compatible. This in turn raises the question, "Who determines what constitutes 'international standards'?" Human rights activists argue that secular international law must be accepted by the entire world as the highest legal standard. Religious activists argue that they owe obedience first and foremost to religious law, and that man-made laws cannot and should not override divine revelation.

Three approaches to the place of Islamic law in Muslim societies continue to be found among Muslims. The first maintains that religious law is outdated and incompatible with modern needs. Thus, Western secular law should be adopted and religious law completely eradicated. The second asserts that what is needed is a more literal restoration of the classical Islamic legal tradition. The third seeks to use the tools or methods of Islamic law to reinterpret and apply Islamic principles and values in developing new legislation to address the needs of modern society. In many Muslim societies today, there is a demand for greater Islamization of the law with the aim of creating legal and judicial systems that are more "authentic" and "legitimate."

Discussion of Islamic law and of Muslim family law raises questions about theory versus practice or legal texts versus the application of law. This volume is concerned with Muslim family law itself—its classical formulation and modern reforms—rather than its specific application by courts. Many women's activists today see the more important initial goal as reform of actual law, with a "trickle down" effect that influences actual practice produced by educating women about their rights and seeking enforcement of law by the courts.

A major development since the 1980s is the rise of women activists and organizations seeking legal reforms. Some, assuming a secular perspective, argue for total eradication of Islamic law in favor of Western, secular law, maintaining that Islamic law does not guarantee equality between genders. Others work within the system, asserting their right to interpret Islam and arguing for reforms on the basis of the intent and the spirit of *Quranic* injunctions. Rejecting the patriarchy of the past and present, as well as the predominant role of the *ulama* (religious scholars), they assert the right of

Muslim women to participate along with men in interpreting religion and religious law.

Change in educational and economic status has played a significant role in the greater empowerment of women. The major goal of the modernization and development plans of the 1950s and 1960s was education and employment of women. In a number of Muslim countries, including Egypt, Syria, and Iraq, women began to work outside the home in increasing numbers. During the 1970s and 1980s, rising numbers of migrant laborers headed to the Gulf, typically leaving wives and children behind. While some sent money back home, women and minors were left without a male guardian to deal with financial and legal matters. In many countries, women's contribution to the financial support of families has been necessary to ensure survival. Consequently, some seek reforms in the patriarchal structure that would create shared rights that reflect shared responsibilities. Rights are tied to responsibilities; the unequal distribution of rights should not continue to exist when responsibilities are shared.

A rising number of women scholars and women's organizations have taken on the challenge of *Quran* and *hadith* interpretation by inserting themselves into a domain that has traditionally belonged to men. Many approach questions of women's status and women's rights in Islam from within the classical tradition and based upon Islamic sources, rather than from a Western or secular perspective. Proceeding from within rather than from "outside" the Islamic tradition can be an effective means of mobilizing popular support and avoiding accusations that they seek to westernize Muslim societies. Factors contributing to women's involvement in scriptural interpretation include rising female literacy and educational levels; women's participation in national struggles such as those in Iran and Kuwait, leading to demands for greater freedom and equality; access to religious education, either in the mosque or in women's study groups; and rising female employment outside the home, which grants women greater financial independence and the opportunity to interact with other women and contribute to the demand for equal status and legal rights.

This second edition of *Women in Muslim Family Law* both updates and expands coverage of modern reforms. Whereas the focus in the first edition was a comparative study of Egypt and Pakistan, this volume introduces a broader comparative perspective, drawing on examples of major reforms in marriage, divorce, and inheritance from the Middle East, South Asia and Southeast Asia. In order to retain the integrity of the volume and in consideration of the limitations of space, no attempt has been made to provide global and exhaustive coverage. Rather, the intent is to identify and discuss significant variations from diverse Muslim contexts. I have made one additional change; I have used Majid Fakhry (tr.), *The Quran: A Modern English Version* (Reading: England, 1999) for *Quranic* quotations.

I am pleased that many have found *Women in Muslim Family Law* useful throughout the years, and that it continues to be cited by colleagues and used as a text in courses. The second edition will enhance its usefulness and demonstrate the ongoing significance of family law in Islam and in gender relations in the Muslim world.

More than twenty years ago, my wife, Jean, played a major role in my completing *Women in Muslim Family Law,* a role she has continued to play in so many ways throughout the thirty-five years of our marriage. This revision would never have been possible, given my other commitments, without the remarkable efforts of Natana J. DeLong-Bas, my extremely talented and tireless research assistant. To both I remain indebted.

Washington, D.C.   John L. Esposito
April 2001

Preface to the First Edition

ARAB OIL and the specter of the Islamic resurgence during the 1970s have focused attention on the Muslim world in a way unparalleled in modern times. The Islamic revival occurring in most Muslim countries has manifested itself at both the personal and political levels. Along with increased mosque attendance, concern for more Islamic forms of dress, and a proliferation of religious literature, Islam has also re-emerged in Muslim politics. Islam is used by governments to legitimate their rule and policies, and it also serves as an umbrella for opposition forces who seek to topple "un-Islamic governments." While Iran has received the greatest media attention, variations on this theme may be found in Pakistan, Saudi Arabia, Egypt, Syria, and Malaysia.

Although profound differences between one Muslim country and another exist, common factors in the Islamic revival include a growing disillusionment with the West, a tendency to blame westernization and secularization for the social disruption and moral decline that has accompanied modernization, and the desire to provide more cultural continuity between modernity and tradition. While past sociopolitical change is seen as a process of critical imitation of the West, the call today is for modernization that is more self-consciously rooted in Islamic history, beliefs, and values. This concern to follow a path of cultural adaptation, rather than to displace the old through a wholesale adoption of the new, raises the practical questions: Does Islam (the Islamic tradition) possess the resources to support and sustain reinterpretation and reform, and thus respond effectively to the demands of modernity? Is Islamic reform possible? What does this mean for women and the family?

Muslim family law provides the primary example of Islamic reform in the twentieth century. Islamic law (the *Shariah*) constitutes the ideal blueprint for Muslim society. It is a divinely revealed law, a comprehensive legal system whose laws govern duties to God *(ibadat,* ritual observances such as prayer, almsgiving, fasting) and duties to one's fellow man *(muamalat,* social transactions which include commercial, penal, and family laws).

Reflecting the centrality of the family in Islam, family law has been the heart of the *Shariah* and the major area of Islamic law that has remained in force to govern the lives of more than 800 million Muslims from North Africa to Southeast Asia. While most areas of Islamic law have been replaced by modern Western legal codes, Muslim family law has provided the major area of Islamic reform.

Change in family law, then, is significant both as an index of social change and as an illustration of Islamic reform, its methodology, and problems. Traditionally, the primary roles of the Muslim woman have been those of wife and mother, living within the extended family in a patriarchal society. Islamic laws set the standards regarding women's rights and duties; modern reforms have been advocated as seeking to protect and improve women's status and rights in a changing society with its movement from the extended family to a more nuclear family. Therefore, among the fundamental questions which Muslims face are: Can Islam change? Can change embody an Islamic rationale that reflects continuity between an Islamic past and modern reforms?

Although studies of family law reform exist, they do not provide the background (development of traditional family law) and context (traditional status of women and the family) necessary for understanding the significance of modern reforms. Secondly, Western scholarship has generally approached the subject from without rather than from within, exploring the resources of the Islamic tradition to supply a rationale and systematic methodology for Islamic reform.

This study will first discuss the historical and legal context for reform (the origins, development, and content of Islamic law). It will then analyze the process, methodology, and extent of modern legal reforms, focusing on changes in Egypt and Pakistan, countries that lend themselves to comparison and contrast. Both countries officially follow the same traditional school of Islamic law (Hanafi), and both were initiators of family law reform, Moreover, in both Egypt and Pakistan, strong movements to establish more Islamically oriented societies have surfaced. The introduction of more Islamic law has become an important issue in Egyptian and Pakistani politics. A major aspect of this effort to establish an Islamic identity more firmly has been a re-examination of the question: What does it mean to be a Muslim woman? This is reflected in women's return to more traditional Islamic forms of dress and behavior, as well as calls for the repeal of certain aspects of family law reform that are seen as un-Islamic. However, significant differences between the Egyptian and Pakistani experiences exist, both in the extent of reform and the legal methodology utilized.

Reform efforts in each country exemplify and illustrate the major legal approaches employed thus far in the Muslim world, as well as the problems and issues surrounding Islamic reform. Where relevant, major family law reforms from other parts of the Muslim world will also be discussed to provide a total picture of the changing status of Muslim women and the possibilities for legal reform. Finally, this study will delineate those dynamic resources in the Islamic tradition that can provide a methodology for future reforms that responds to the continued and changing needs of Muslim society.

While this study is inescapably technical in nature, it has been organized and written to accommodate the nonspecialists as well as the specialists. Diacritical marks have been omitted to simplify reading and to reduce production costs. A brief bibliography has been included for further reading.

I am indebted to Ismail R. al-Faruqi (Temple University) and Hassan Hanafi (Cairo University) for my early training in Islamic Studies and for their many helpful comments and observations throughout the years. Several typists—Barbara Letourneau, Lorna Mattus, Elizabeth Stebbins, and Kathleen Lauring—have worked on successive versions of this manuscript. Finally, my wife Jean, my parents, and brothers have been and continue to be an inestimable source of inspiration and support.

Worcester, Massachusetts   JLE
Summer 1981

Women in Muslim Family Law

1 The Sources of Islamic Law

THE CENTRAL FACT of the Muslim religious experience is Allah (God). In contrast to the polytheism of pre-Islamic Arabia, the God of the *Quran* is one and transcendent: "And your God is One God: there is no God but He, the Compassionate, the Merciful" (2:163). This God, the creator and sustainer of the universe, is the overwhelming concern of the believer.[1] Man's duty is obedience and submission *(islam)* to the will of God. The submission incumbent upon the Muslim, however, is not that of mere passivity; rather, it is submission to the Divine imperative, to actively realize God's will in history. Thus, the *Quran* declares that man is God's vicegerent on earth (2:30; 35:39). God has given him the Divine Trust *(amanah)* (33:72; 6:165), and it is on the basis of how man executes his vicegerency that he is to be either rewarded or punished (6:165).

Man's obligation to realize the divine imperative in space and time is communal as well as individual. The Islamic community *(ummah)* is to be the dynamic vehicle for the realization of the divine pattern (3:110; 2:148; 58:109; 103:2–3), and, as such, the *ummah* is to serve as an example to other peoples of the world (2:143; 6:72; 10:45–46).

The Muslim concern not simply to know the divine will but also to execute it inspired the early Muslim community's expansion and conquest of Arabia, the Eastern Byzantine Empire in Palestine, Syria, Lebanon, the Persian (Sasanid) Empire in Iran and Iraq, and Egypt. However, the realization of the Muslims' religious vision to transform the world was not a simple task. The geographical expansion of Islam resulted in many new problems, which raised the question, "How is the divine will to be realized in this situation?" Because the *Quran* is not a law book (i.e., not a collection of pre-

1

scriptions providing a legal system) and because the Prophet was no longer alive to resolve problems, the early Caliphs, and later, during the Umayyad period (661–750), the judges *(qadis)* shouldered the responsibility of rendering legal decisions.

In the eighth century, owing to a growing dissatisfaction with Umayyad rule and a belief that its courts had failed to incorporate and implement the spirit of *Quranic* reforms, early schools of law *(madhhab,* pl. *madhahib)* emerged in major cities of the empire. These schools originally consisted of pious Muslims in Mecca, Medina, Kufa, and Baghdad. In time, they attracted followers who associated themselves with one of the great early leaders *(imams)*—men like Abu Hanifa (d. 767), Malik ibn Anas (d. 796), Muhammad ibn Idris al-Shafii (d. 820), and Ahmad ibn Hanbal (d. 855)—who came to be viewed respectively as the founders of the Hanafi, Maliki, Shafii, and Hanbali schools. While there were originally many schools of law, only these four survived over time.[2]

Because of the breadth of the *ummah* and the varying cultural practices that it embraced, as well as the number of law schools, many differences existed both in the legal techniques employed and the substantive law that developed. Muhammad ibn Idris al-Shafii (d. 204/820), the father of Muslim jurisprudence, sought to systematize the methodology of the law schools and thus limit the growing diversity in Islamic law. Al-Shafii came at a critical time in Muslim history. His actions brought about the culmination of long-term conflicts between two schools of legal thought. The first relied on the free use of reasoned opinions *(ahl al-ray)* of the ancient schools, while the second, the traditionist *(ahl al-hadith),* relied upon the *Quran* and the *Sunnah* of the Prophet as the only valid sources of legal doctrine. The traditionist movement criticized the *ahl al-ray* schools for their dependence on the practice of their own school and for their free exercise of personal opinion *(ray)* because it produced too much diversity of doctrine. To meet the need for a more systematic legal method, al-Shafii, who deplored the great variety of doctrine, sought to limit the sources of law *(usul al-fiqh),* and thereby establish a common methodology for all schools of law. As a result of his efforts, by the ninth century, the classical theory of law fixed the sources of Islamic law at four: the *Quran,* the *Sunnah* of the Prophet, *qiyas* (analogical reasoning), and *ijma* (consensus).

The Sources of Islamic Law

THE *Quran*

The *Quran* is the revelation of God, the central fact of the Islamic religious experience. As the very word of God, for Muslims the *Quran* is the presence of the numinous in history (space and time).

Quranic revelation is not that of the transcendent God, but rather of his Divine Will, which man is to follow: "This is a declaration for mankind, a guidance and admonition for the God-fearing" (3:138). Thus, the primary material source of the revealed law is quite naturally the *Holy Quran,* the source book of Islamic values. While the *Quran* does contain prescriptions about matters that would rank as legal in the strict, narrow sense of the term, these injunctions, in fact, comprise but eighty verses. The bulk of *Quranic* matter consists mainly of broad, general moral directives as to what the aims and aspirations of Muslims should be, the "ought" of the Islamic religious ethic.

The *Quran* was revealed to Muhammad over a period of twenty-three years in order to meet the needs of the Islamic society in Mecca and then in Medina. It gradually provided an Islamic ideology for the community and, in the process, modified or supplemented existing customs not meeting Islamic standards.

Those verses most important for the development of legal doctrine came about in Medina during the growth of the community-state. Verses were revealed that replaced or revised old tribal customs with new rules. The gradual replacement of existing customs that did not meet Islamic standards is well illustrated by the *Quranic* prohibitions of liquor and games of chance. The use of alcohol and gambling were not prohibited in the early years and, hence, the old custom continued to be followed. The first prescription against the old custom is given in the form of advice: "They ask you concerning wine and gambling, say: In both is great sin and some benefit for people; but the sin is greater than the benefit" (2:219). Later, Muslims were prohibited from offering prayers in drunkenness: "O believers, do not approach prayer while you are drunk, until you know what you say" (4:43). Later still, liquor and gambling were fully prohibited, with the explanation: "The Devil

3

only wishes to stir up enmity and hatred among you, through wine and gambling, and keep you away from remembering God and from prayer. Will you not desist, then?" (5:91).

Some of the most important and fundamental reforms of customary law introduced in the *Quran* were designed to improve the status of women and strengthen the family in Muslim society. Three main areas of *Quranic* reform were marriage, divorce, and inheritance. In the realm of marriage, for example, the Quran commands that only the wife and not her father or other male relatives should receive the dower *(mahr)* from her husband: "And give women their dowers as a free gift" (4:4). Thus, the woman becomes a legal partner to the marriage contract rather than an object for sale. In addition, unlimited polygamy was curtailed and the number of wives limited to four. However, a final injunction stressed that if the husband did not believe that he could be equally fair to each of his wives, he should marry only one: "Marry such of the women as appeal to you, two, three or four; but if you fear that you cannot be equitable, then only one" (4:3). Elsewhere, the *Quran* continues: "You will never be able to treat wives equitably, even if you are bent on doing that" (4:129).

In the area of divorce, *Quranic* reforms provide an opportunity for reconciliation. An important reform calls for a waiting period *(iddah)* of three months, or, if a wife is pregnant, until delivery of her child, before her husband can divorce her: "As for those of your women who have despaired of menstruation, if you are in doubt, then their term shall be three months; and those too who have not menstruated yet. As to those women with child, their term shall be upon delivering their burden" (65:4).

Inheritance provides another example of *Quranic* reform of existing practice. The advent of Islam brought a shift from tribal allegiance to the solidarity of the *ummah*, a brotherhood of believers that was to transcend all tribal and racial loyalties. Coupled with this shift was a concern for the strength of the family and the members within it, especially women. These concerns are exemplified in the *Quranic* regulations governing inheritance. In tribal customary law, succession was based solely on an agnatic system *(asabah)*, i.e., kinship, and thus inheritance, through male descent. The *Quran* modified this system by introducing the golden rule of inheritance, the primacy of distribution of certain fixed shares to several categories of designated heirs comprised mainly of the nearest female relatives excluded under the agnatic system. After these *Quranic* claims have been satisfied, the residue of the estate is awarded to the nearest male relatives.

THE *Sunnah* OF THE PROPHET

Quranic values were concretized and interpreted by the second material source of law, the *Sunnah* of the Prophet. Just as Muslims turned to the Prophet for decisions during his lifetime, so after his death they looked to his example for guidance. In classical theory, the *Sunnah* of the Prophet consists quite simply in the normative model behavior of the Prophet. The importance of the *Sunnah* of the Prophet is rooted in the *Quranic* command to obey and follow Muhammad: "O believers, obey God and obey His Apostle . . . Should you quarrel over any matter, then refer it to God and the Apostle" (4:59), and again, "You have had a good example in God's Apostle, for him who hopes for God and the Last Day and remembers God often" (33:21). Technically, *Sunnah* is divided into three categories: (1) *al-sunnah al-qawliyah,* the Prophet's statements and sayings; (2) *al-sunnah al-filiyah,* his deeds; and (3) *al-sunnah al-taqririyah,* his silent or tacit approval of certain deeds of which he had knowledge.

The record of the Prophetic words and deeds is to be found in the narrative reports or traditions *(hadith)* transmitted and finally collected and recorded in compendia. The authoritative collections of *hadith* were not compiled until the middle of the ninth century, by which time a great mass of diverse *hadiths* reflected the variety of legal opinion developed over the previous two centuries of juristic reasoning in the legal schools. Recognition that the *hadith* literature included fabrications led to a concerted effort by scholars to distinguish more clearly the authentic traditions.

The *hadiths* were evaluated through a painstaking effort that produced the new Muslim science of *hadith* criticism *(mustalah al-hadith)*. Criteria were established for judging the trustworthiness of narrators. For example, they had to be adult Muslims, legally responsible, of good moral reputation (rational, just, moral), and known to have good memories. Then a link-by-link examination of the chain of transmission was made to trace the continuity of the tradition back to the Prophet.

On the basis of such examination of the chain of narrators, *hadiths* were generally classified from the point of view of narration as *mutawatir* (continuous), *mashhur* (well-known), and *ahad* (isolated). *Mutawatir* refers to a tradition whose chain of narrators *(isnad)* is consistent and continuous. *Mashhur* refers to those traditions that were widely disseminated and whose narration could be traced back to one or two narrators in the time of the Prophet. *Ahad* refers to traditions whose last link *(sanad)* in the chain of narrators was limited to one authority. This last category was inferior to the first two and was therefore considered weaker. The three categories were divided into subcategories to further distinguish the strength or weakness of traditions.

The second criteria for judging the *hadith,* an examination of its matter *(matn),* involved asking if this matter contradicted the *Quran,* a verified tradition, reason, or the consensus of the community. After the traditions had been subjected to both external (narrators) and internal (subject matter) examination, they were labeled according to the degree of their strength or authenticity as *sahih* (authentic), *hasan* (good), or *daif* (weak). Of the six major collections of *hadith* of the Prophet, the *Sahihs* of Muhammad ibn Ismail al-Bukhari (d. 870) and that of Muslim ibn al-Hajjaj (d. 875) have enjoyed an especially high reputation. However, as shall be discussed in Chapter 4, questions regarding the authenticity of the *hadith* remained.

Qiyas

Muslims' concern to be true to the material sources *(Quran* and *Sunnah* of the Prophet) of their faith led to the development of *qiyas,* the third source of law. *Qiyas* is a restricted form of *ijtihad* (personal reasoning or interpretation); it is reasoning by analogy. The noted jurist Shihab al-Din al-Qarafi (d. 1285) defined *qiyas* as "establishing the relevance of a ruling in one case to another case because of a similarity in the attribute (reason or cause) upon which the ruling was based."[3]

The key to the use of *qiyas* is the discovery of the *illa* (reason or effective cause) for a *Shariah* rule. If a similar *illa* was judged to be present in the new case under consideration, then the *Shariah* judgment was applied. Among the earliest usages of *qiyas* was the fixing of the minimum dower. An analogy was established between the loss of virginity following marriage and the *Quranic* penalty for theft—amputation of the hand. The sums of the minimum dower in Kufa and in Medina were equivalent to the established values that stolen goods had to reach in Kufan and Medinan teaching, respectively, before amputation was applicable.[4]

Ijma

The fourth source of law, *ijma*, has played a key role in the development of Islamic law. The classical and standard definition of *ijma* is the unanimous agreement of the jurists of a particular age on a specific issue. *Ijma* derived its authority as a source of law from the *hadith* that records the Prophet as saying, "My Community will never agree on an error."

In the early community, *ijma* was not a formalized practice. It developed after the death of Muhammad and the consequent loss of his guidance in legislative matters. *Ijma* began as a natural process for solving problems and making decisions, depending upon the approval of majority opinion to insure against the fallibility of individual reasoning.

Two kinds of *ijma* should be distinguished. The *ijma al-ummah* refers to the consensus of the whole community. It is used in matters of religious practice, for example, the ritual of pilgrimage to Mecca that is practiced by all pilgrims. However, authority for this *ijma* is not found in early legal texts. The second type, *ijma al-aimmah*, meets the classical definition of a consensus of religious authorities regarding interpretation of a *Quranic* text or tradition, or a development of legal principle.

Ijma contributed significantly to the corpus of law *(fiqh)*. If questions arose about a *Quranic* text or tradition, or a problem for which no *sunnah* (practice) of the community existed, the jurists applied their own reasoning *(ijtihad)* to arrive at an interpretation. Over a period of time (perhaps several generations), one interpretation came to be accepted by more and more doctors of law. Looking back in time at the evolved consensus of the scholars, it could be concluded that an *ijma* of scholars had been reached on the issue.

The general consensus of Muslim jurists *(faqih,* pl. *fuqaha)* has always been that the *Shariah* is concerned with human welfare and based upon justice and equity. The four Sunni schools of law developed and utilized the following subsidiary legal methods whose primary purpose was the guaranteeing of justice and equity: *istihsan* (juristic preference), *istislah* (public interest), and *istishab* (presumption of continuity). All are considered forms of *ijtihad.*

Istihsan

Istihsan is a principle associated with the Hanafi school. Where strict analogical reasoning led to an unnecessarily harsh or rigid result, juristic preference was exercised to achieve equity. Proponents of this principle could cite the *Quran* to support their position: "Those who hear the Word and follow the fairest of it; those are the ones whom God has guided and those are the people of understanding!" (39:18) and "And follow the fairest of what has been sent down to you from your Lord" (39: 55). The Shafiis completely rejected this principle.

Istislah

The second supplementary principle of law is *istislah,* a method associated primarily with the Maliki school, but also used by the Hanbalis and Shafiis. *Istislah* is a tool of interpretation and not a material source of substantive law. It is based on the belief that God's purpose in the *Shariah* is the promotion of human welfare. Public interest or human welfare *(maslahah)* was accepted as a source of law, provided that the case was suitable and relevant to either a universal legal principle or specific textual evidence. Although not textually specified *(mursal),* public interests *(al-masalih al-mursalah)* can be served by determining what is in a person's or the community's best interest in a case and rendering a judgment that will promote it.

Istislah was not simply utilitarian; it did not develop as a freewheeling practice, but rather as a disciplined principle of law with definite limits within which it was to function. The case involved must be one that concerns social transactions *(muamalat)*, rather than religious observances *(ibadat)*, and the determination of public interest must be in harmony with the spirit of the *Shariah*.

Istishab

Istishab, continuance or permanence, is a principle of equity most often associated with the Shafiis, although it was also emphasized by the Hanbalis. The term *istishab* refers to the presumption in the law that conditions known to exist in the past continue to exist or remain valid until proven otherwise. For example, a missing person *(mafqud)* is presumed to be alive until the opposite is established, either through proof of his demise or a judicial decree to that effect based on the elapsing of the number of years necessary to complete a normal life span.

The history of Islamic law contains numerous examples of Muslim sovereigns interpreting and enacting laws in view of justice or the general welfare. Such actions were founded in the very sources of law: the *Quran*, the *Sunnah* of the Prophet, *qiyas*, and *ijma*.

Conclusion

The early Muslims' religious vision of realizing the Will of God in history inspired not only the vast geographical expansion of Islam but also the early development of Islamic law. The concern about knowing God's Will in order to implement it produced classical Muslim law. The science of Muslim jurisprudence within these first centuries devised both the sources of law *(usul al-fiqh)* and substantive law itself *(furu al-fiqh)*. As we have seen, according to classical legal theory that has predominated down to the twentieth century, in the development of law, four sources of jurisprudence were employed: the *Quran*, the *Sunnah* of the Prophet, *qiyas*, and *ijma*. Laws were derived from the revealed texts of the *Quran* and the *Sunnah*, or from the product of the jurists' analogical reasoning based upon these texts. The authority for their interpretations came from what was considered the infallible *ijma* of the scholars. At the same time, there was recognition within the schools themselves of subsidiary principles of equity *(istihsan, istislah,* and *istishab).*

However, because of a number of factors, the interaction of these sources and the dynamism of legal development were stifled after the tenth century. A series of events—debates about whether or not the door of *ijtihad* had closed, growing political fragmentation and decay, assimilated customs contrary to the *Quranic* spirit, and finally the Mongol invasions of the thirteenth century—all played a part in halting creative legal activity.

The relationship between *ijtihad* and *ijma* had, during the formative period of law, been a dynamic one in which the fresh *ijtihad* (interpretation) of the scholar was either accepted or rejected by the community. In the twelfth century, however, a majority of Hanafi legal scholars determined that the elaboration of the law was essentially complete. The Hanafis thus deemed that independent interpretation was no longer necessary and encouraged jurists instead to follow, or imitate *(taqlid),* the established authoritative doctrines of the Hanafi law school. By contrast, the Hanbali and a minority of Shafii jurists continued to practice *ijtihad,* believing it to be a required duty of the Muslim community.

By the thirteenth century, the Hanafis, Malikis and the majority of Shafiis accepted that a *muqallid* (a person who adheres to *taqlid)* could function as a jurisconsult, encouraging the practice of following past rulings, rather than maintaining the historical dynamic relationship between *ijtihad* and *ijma. Ijma* thus became the infallible consensus of scholars and, as such, functioned in legal theory as an instrument of legal conservatism. As will be discussed later, it was, in part, this emphasis on *taqlid* and denial of the right to exercise *ijtihad* that led to the religious revivals of the eighteenth century which were precursors to the modernist and Islamist movements of the nineteenth and twentieth centuries.

The effect of legal conservatism is reflected in the legal literature of the period, which largely consisted of exhaustive commentaries on the principal works of the great *Imams* of the past, most notably Abu Hanifa, Malik, al-Shafii, and Ibn Hanbal. These legal handbooks contained the principal teachings of each school of law and served as authoritative reference works for the *qadis* (judges) who applied the law.

Among the other factors contributing to Muslim conservatism was the growing political fragmentation of the Abbasid Caliphate from the middle of the tenth century, a gradual decentralization into small semi-autonomous feudal states. This period of political decline was accompanied by a growing moral and social decay as the Muslim ruling class, in addition to its earlier absorptions of Byzantine and Persian governmental institutions, assimilated many of their less savory practices—large harems, concubines, and, most important for women's role in the family, the customs of veiling and seclusion.[5]

Political weakness produced a steady decline of the Abbasid dynasty and culminated in its collapse in 1258 at the hands of the Mongols. The Mongol invaders led by Hulagu Khan destroyed the cultural centers of the eastern Muslim world, including mosque-universities and libraries, and killed hundreds of thousands of the region's inhabitants. The response of the Muslim community amidst this collapse was a withdrawal into conservatism and resistance to change. Unfortunately, many of the practices of the time, which had resulted from the acculturation of foreign customs and pre-Islamic traditions which were contrary to *Quranic* values, were already associated with religion, and thus were preserved. This conservative reaction, coupled with the claim that the "door to *ijtihad*" had been closed in legal matters in favor of *taqlid,* resulted in the relative stagnation of the Muslim community and its jurisprudence.

These sources of conservatism contributed to the rather static character of Muslim society and law in the medieval period, a situation that persisted up to the eighteenth century, when calls began for the revival, renewal, and reform of Islam, particularly the radical rejection of *taqlid* in favor of *ijtihad*. This perspective gave rise to debates about the compatibility between Islam and modernity in the nineteenth century, culminating in further calls in the twentieth century for Islamic reform and the revival of the dynamism of Islamic law, with particular emphasis on modern social conditions, public interest, and focusing on the spirit, rather than the letter, of the law. A discussion of modern family law reforms that have been proposed and passed as a result will follow in Chapters 3 and 4.

2 Classical Muslim Family Law

FAMILY LAW, which includes such important areas as marriage, divorce and succession, has enjoyed pride of place within the *Shariah*, a prominence that reflects the *Quranic* concern for the rights of women and the family. Thus, the traditional family social structure, as well as the roles and responsibilities of its members and family values, may be identified in the law.

As noted in Chapter 1, the *Quran* introduced substantial reforms affecting the position of women by creating new regulations and modifying existing customary practice. These *Quranic* reforms, as well as customary practice, constitute the substance of classical Muslim family law.

Where *Quranic* reforms and values were incorporated, they served to raise the status of women and the family in Muslim society by establishing the rights of family members. In order to provide a background against which *Quranic* reforms and customary influences can be appreciated, this chapter will begin with a survey of women and the family in pre-Islamic Arabia. This survey will be followed by a presentation of the major regulations for marriage, divorce, and inheritance in classical family law according to the Hanafi school, which is the predominant official school of Islamic law in the Middle East and South Asia.

Women in Pre-Islamic Arabia

Although pre-Islamic poetry and other sources indicate that several types of marriage—patrilineal/patrilocal, patriarchal, matrilineal/matrilocal, uxorilocal, polyandrous, and polygamous—probably existed in pre-Islamic Arabia, the predominant pattern was patrilineal/patrilocal (i.e., a woman was placed under the control of her husband and lived with him and his tribe). Women were not necessarily subservient to men. Some strong women did receive tribute in poetry but women in general are not prominent in pre-Islamic literature. Examples exist of women who conducted their own marriages, participated in business ventures, entered into contracts, and owned and managed property, such as Muhammad's first wife, Khadijah. However, female participation in these ventures was typically contingent upon male permission and support. Moreover, it is unclear how widespread these practices were, particularly in the time period immediately preceding Muhammad.

In matters of marriage, a woman's most important assets were her sexual purity and reproductive capacities. Because a man, who owned property, needed to be certain that his heirs were truly his children, the question of female chastity and fidelity was a point of honor for the prospective bride's family, raising the value of female virginity. In the predominant patrilineal/patrilocal pattern of marriage, the wife—and the children she would bear—became the property of her husband. Her own tribe relinquished its claim to the wife and to the children she would bear in exchange for the payment of a dower *(mahr)*.

Consequently, a woman's value to her tribe came to rest primarily on the amount of the dower it could expect to receive upon her marriage. As a wife, a woman became subject to her husband and his kindred and totally dependent upon them for maintenance and support. In addition, a woman's right to inheritance from her own family, especially of fixed property such as land, which would in effect mean transferring family wealth to another tribe, was out of the question. However, she maintained her blood kinship to her own tribe and had the right to their protection in the event that her husband mistreated her.

Women's low status in society is reflected in the *Quranic* condemnations of various practices, especially the prohibitions of levirate (forcing a widowed woman to marry her husband's brother, essentially rendering her a part of the estate) and female infanticide. As the *Quran* notes of the birth of female children: "And if the birth of a daughter is announced to any of them, his face turns black, and he is enraged. He hides from the people on account of the evil news broken to him; should he keep it in humiliation or bury it in the ground? Evil is what they judge!" (16:58–59).[1]

Another factor contributing to women's inferior status was men's right of unlimited polygamy, contingent solely upon the male's ability to capture or purchase women. Furthermore, there was no waiting period after divorce in pre-Islamic Arabia. Some scholars argue that this gave women greater freedom to pursue immediate remarriage and greater control over their own sexuality and reproductive functions. However, it should also be noted that the lack of a waiting period was accompanied by a lack of maintenance after the divorce, so that a woman who did not immediately remarry might find herself in severe financial straits, especially if she happened to be pregnant.

These factors provide the social context against which the life of Muhammad and the revelation of the *Quran* must be understood in order to see the profound changes wrought by Islam.

Islam brought a shift in the basis of the social foundation—from blood kinship to fellowship in a community *(ummah)* of believers, from loyalty to the tribe to a focus on the extended family as the basic social unit. An emphasis on family strength meant recognition not only of male rights but of female rights as well. This realization can be seen in family law reforms in the areas of marriage, divorce and inheritance. *Quranic* injunctions intended to raise women's status and foster equality represented some of the most radical departures from customary law in ancient Arabia.

Marriage

WHY MARRIAGE?

The central role of marriage in Islam is well illustrated by the Prophet's oft-quoted statement that "There shall be no monkery in Islam." Islam considers marriage, which is an important safeguard for chastity, to be incumbent on every Muslim man and woman unless they are physically or financially unable to pursue conjugal life. Through marriage, the Muslim engages in an activity that is life-affirming rather than life-denying. Marriage is central to the growth and stability of the basic unit of society, the Muslim family, the

14

means by which the world is populated with Muslims to concretize and realize God's Will in history by spreading the faith and fighting for it.

DEFINITION OF MARRIAGE

Marriage *(nikah)* in Islam is recognized as a highly religious sacred covenant. However, it is not religious in the sense of a sacrament, but rather in the sense of realizing the essence of Islam. In Islamic law, marriage is a civil contract legalizing intercourse and procreation. Marriage, reflecting the practical bent of Islam, combines the nature of both *ibadat* (worship) and *muamalat* (social relations).

ESSENTIAL REQUIREMENTS OF MARRIAGE

The contractual nature of marriage in Islam makes the woman a party to the marriage agreement, rather than an object of sale. Islamic law requires the consent of the adult woman to the marriage. A Muslim man or woman who is of sound mind and who has attained puberty (in classical law, twelve years of age for boys and nine years for girls) is considered to be legally eligible for marriage. Because it was customary in an agrarian society to marry at an early age, the sanctioning of marriage at puberty was appropriate to the social situation. Great emphasis was placed on the value of many children, which a young wife with many child-bearing years ahead could more easily provide.

Muslim men of legal majority are permitted to contract their own marriages. Muslim women typically must have a male guardian contract their marriage for them. The Hanafi school of Islamic law theoretically allows a woman of legal majority to contract her own marriage, although this practice does not appear to have been widespread. In order for such a marriage to be considered legally valid, the prospective husband must be of equal social status and piety, and the woman must demand the proper dower. If she does not demand the proper dower, her male guardian has the right to demand that the proper dower be paid or that the marriage be dissolved.

The law does not require any particular form or ceremony in which the contractual agreement must be made, nor does it require any evidence of the union in writing. The custom of oral contracts seems to have prevailed, although the *Quran* does recommend that such an agreement be in written form: "Let a scribe write it for you with fairness. No scribe should decline to write as God has taught him . . . This is more equitable in God's sight, more suitable for testimony and less likely to rouse your doubts" (2:282).

Essential to the marriage is the offer *(ijab)* of one contracting party and the acceptance *(qabul)* of the other, occurring at the same meeting before two witnesses. In Islamic law, by *Quranic* provision, the place of one male witness may be taken by two female witnesses: "And call to witness two witnesses of your men; if not two men, then one man and two women from such witnesses you approve of, so that if one of them fails to remember, the other would remind her" (2:282). The higher social regard for men as witnesses in worldly affairs is reflected in the above regulation. This higher regard for men results in granting them more extensive rights in the law. In laws governing the arrangement of marriage for minors, the rights of men and women, as well as boys and girls, differ considerably.

GUARDIANSHIP IN MARRIAGE

A distinguishing feature of Islamic law is the power *(jabr)* that it bestows upon the father or grandfather, who can contract a valid marriage for minors that cannot be annulled at puberty. The right of guardianship is known as *wilayat* and the guardian is a *wali*. The inability of minors to repudiate the marriage seems to rest on the jurists' assumption that fathers and grandfathers who are fond of their offspring would not have sinister motives in arranging marriages. However, this regulation is not supported by any *Quranic* prescription or *Sunnah* of the Prophet. If the marriage is contracted negligently or fraudulently, or by someone other than the father or grandfather, the minor may exercise the "option of puberty" *(khiyar al-bulugh)* and repudiate the marriage upon attaining puberty. The option applies to all marriages contracted by anyone other than the father or grandfather, including the minor's mother, who, as a woman, may be "deficient in judgment."[2]

Lack of confidence in a woman's judgment is an attitude (also reflected in Western countries for many centuries) that probably resulted from the strict division of labor and social activity in Muslim society. The woman who spent most of her life engaged in domestic duties, completely segregated from the world of legal and business agreements, came to be viewed as less competent to deal with such matters. Thus, one can see the influence of custom and traditional attitudes upon the law. Among the many illustrations found in family law are the rules governing the option of puberty. This option is lost to the virgin female who has reached puberty if she takes no action or if she merely remains silent for what is considered a reasonable time after she has been informed of the marriage and of her option. However, the option is preserved for the boy under the same circumstances. His right continues until he actively approves the marriage or implies approval by the act of payment of dower or by actual cohabitation.[3]

If the husband or wife does exercise the option to repudiate a marriage, it must be confirmed by the court. Until such confirmation, the marriage continues, and if either party should die in the interval, the other would inherit from him or her.

CLASSIFICATION OF MARRIAGE

Like all other contracts, marriage has certain qualifications. However, unless its most basic requirements are violated, its validity remains. Marriages are classified by the degree of their validity as (a) *batil*, void, completely bad in its foundations; (b) *fasid*, irregular, good in its foundations but unlawful in its attributes; and (c) *sahih*, valid and completely lawful. As will be indicated, those marriage partners who do not fulfill all legal requirements for a *sahih* marriage are, in turn, denied many important legal rights.

Batil *Marriage*

A *batil* (void) marriage is an unlawful union that awards no mutual rights to the partners and imposes no obligations. The death of one partner does not entitle the other to any inheritance. Because the marriage is null and void and thus not considered to exist, the offspring are illegitimate. *Batil* marriages include such situations as marriage of a Muslim woman to more than one husband at the same

17

time, or a marriage prohibited on the grounds of consanguinity (blood relationship through a male ancestor), affinity (marital relationship), or fosterage.

Fasid *Marriage*

A *fasid* marriage is irregular because of (1) lack of a formality that may be rectified, as in the case of a secret marriage or a marriage contracted with less than the legal number of witnesses, or (2) an impediment that can be removed, as when a husband already has four wives. If a judge *(qadi)* is made aware of such an irregular marriage, he, as guardian of the law of God, must either legalize or terminate the relationship.

An irregular marriage has no legal effect until it is consummated, and even after consummation, the rights of the partners are limited. The wife has the right of dower but no right of maintenance. Furthermore, there are no mutual rights of inheritance. The children of this marriage are considered legitimate, however, and are entitled to a share of the inheritance. To dissolve the relationship, only a single declaration of divorce is necessary. One of the partners at any time need only say "I have relinquished you" to annul the contract.

Sahih *Marriage*

A *sahih* (sound or valid) marriage conforms to every requirement of the law and is not affected by prohibitions in the *batil* marriages or in *fasid* marriages. The partners of a *sahih* marriage are entitled to all of the rights and subject to all of the obligations of a valid marriage.

COMPETENCY OF THE PARTIES IN A MARRIAGE

The various requirements that determine the classification of a marriage center around the following areas: (1) number of spouses, (2) religion, (3) family relationship, (4) *iddah,* and (5) equality.

Number of Spouses

A Muslim man may have up to four wives. This law represents another reform raising the status of women, who had been subjected to unlimited polygamy in pre-Islamic times. Social circumstances during the period must be kept in mind, including the widespread acceptance of the practice of polygamy and the existence of many widows and orphans, the wives and children of men who had died in battle, who were in need of protection through marriage. The *Quranic* verse from which the control of polygamy is derived must be understood in the context of problems resulting from the battle of Uhud (625), which had caused the deaths of a substantial percentage of Muslim men: "If you fear that you cannot deal justly with the orphans, then marry such of the women as appeal to you, two, three or four; but if you fear that you cannot be equitable, then only one" (4:3).

Because of the patrilineal social structure through which children belonged to the male's family, a Muslim woman was only permitted to marry one husband at a time so that the paternity of her children could be established. If she married a second husband, this marriage was considered to be completely void. In addition, her children from the second husband were illegitimate and were therefore excluded from inheritance. They could not be legitimized by any later acknowledgment.

Religion

Under Hanafi law, a Muslim man is allowed to marry a Muslim woman, or a Jewish or Christian woman *(kitabiyyah)* who believes in a heavenly or revealed religion that has a *kitab* or revealed book. He cannot, however, marry an idolatress or a fire-worshipper. A Muslim woman, again more controlled in the exercise of her options, can marry only a Muslim man.[4]

Family Relationship

Prohibitions of marriage based on family relationship are derived from the *Quran* (4:23). Marriages are prohibited for partners who have a certain blood relationship or consanguinity. Thus, a man may not marry his ascendants h.h.s. (how high soever) or descendants h.l.s. (how low soever).[5]

A man is also prohibited from marriage with relations by affinity, that is, the ascendants h.h.s. or descendants h.l.s. of his wife (provided his marriage to this wife was consummated) or the wife of an ascendant h.h.s. or descendant h.l.s. Also prohibited is a marriage where the relationship of fosterage exists, for example, marriage with one's foster-sister, foster-mother, or her daughter.

Another barrier to marriage in the category of family relationship involves unlawful conjunction. A Muslim must not be married at the same time to women related by consanguinity, affinity, or fosterage, such as sisters or an aunt and her niece. An unlawful union in Hanafi law renders a marriage irregular but not void.[6]

Iddah

In Hanafi law, a woman is prohibited from remarrying for a specified period of time *(iddah)* in cases where her previous marriage has been terminated by divorce or by the death of her husband. Only after the completion of *iddah* would a new marriage, if contracted, be lawful. During *iddah,* a woman must remain in seclusion in order to ascertain whether she is pregnant by her husband, and thus avoid any confusion of parentage. As will be discussed later, the *iddah* served a number of purposes in addition to determining parentage. It also was a period for reconciliation and required payment of maintenance. If a marriage is not consummated, *iddah* need not be observed, except in the case of a husband's death, because consummation could be the subject of conflicting claims of paternity, inheritance, and maintenance.

If the marriage is consummated before it is dissolved by divorce, the duration of the *iddah* is three menstrual cycles. If the woman is pregnant, the *iddah* continues until her delivery. If the marriage is terminated by the husband's death, the *iddah* period is four months plus ten days from the death of the husband. If, at the conclusion of this period, the widow is pregnant, her *iddah* continues until delivery of the child.

The prohibitions of *iddah* after divorce extend to the husband, who may not marry again during the period of his former wife's *iddah*. However, marriage before the completion of the *iddah* is not considered void, but merely irregular.

To determine consummation of the marriage, which is a key issue in the practice of *iddah*, valid retirement *(al-khalwah al-sahihah)* can be used. To prove valid retirement, the husband and wife must have privacy and there must be no impediment to marital intercourse. Valid retirement also has the same effect as consummation not only in determining *iddah,* but also in confirming the right to dower, in establishing paternity, and in assessing the wife's right to maintenance.

Equality

The doctrine of *kafaah,* or the rule of equality, states that a marriage is a suitable union in law if the man is equal in social status to the woman. This doctrine is typically only a matter of concern if the man is considered to be of lower status than the woman, because a woman is considered to be raised to the husband's position by marriage. In Hanafi law, equality is determined by (1) family, (2) Islam, (3) profession, (4) freedom, (5) good character, and (6) means. A marriage that does not favorably meet these criteria is not necessarily void. The *qadi* must investigate whether the man misrepresented his social status to the prospective bride's family, as well as whether the marriage guardian was responsible for contracting the marriage or whether the woman contracted the marriage herself. The judge must then exercise his own discretion in deciding whether to annul the marriage *(faskh)* on the basis that it was a mésalliance, provided that the woman is not pregnant and that not more than a year has elapsed since the inequality was discovered.

CONSEQUENCES OF MARRIAGE (RIGHTS AND OBLIGATIONS OF PARTNERS)

Once the essential requirements for a valid marriage have been fulfilled, the marriage agreement imposes specific obligations and ensures specific rights for each marriage partner. Among the most significant rights and obligations are those concerning the duties of the wife, regulation of marriage agreements, property, dower, and maintenance rights, guardianship, and parentage.

Duties of the Wife

The wife's main obligation involves maintaining a home, caring for her children, and obeying her husband. He is entitled to exercise his marital authority by restraining his wife's movements and preventing her from showing herself in public. This restriction of the wife mirrors the prevailing medieval social customs of veiling and seclusion of women, practiced in order to protect their honor.

Regulation of Marriage Agreements

The rights guaranteed to a woman as a legal entity under Islam ensure her a certain status before the law and grant her some power in her relationships with men. One important right granted by the Hanbali (but not Hanafi) law school that gives women a certain amount of independence and status in marriage is her right to insert conditions that are favorable to her directly into the marriage contract. The wife's ability to make conditions, provided that they are not contrary to the object of marriage, can resolve many inequities in areas such as polygamy and divorce. For example, clauses may be added that eliminate the husband's right to take a second wife or that grant the wife greater freedom of movement. These conditions limit the husband's somewhat automatic and extensive legal control over his wife. Because these conditions can be enforced by granting the wife her husband's power of divorce if they are violated, they bestow more equal rights of divorce to the wife. As will be seen later, this approach has been incorporated into modern reforms of family law.

Agreements on conditions can be drawn up at the time of the marriage or afterward, and are valid and enforceable provided they are not contrary to the policy of the law. Conditions that are contrary to the object of marriage (for example, clauses saying that the wife need not live with her husband or that the husband need not maintain his wife) would be void, although the marriage would still be valid. However, clauses that extend the natural consequences of marriage, such as a husband's promise to maintain his wife in a certain lifestyle, are valid.

Property Rights

Although each party in a marriage may inherit from the other, neither acquires interest in the property of a spouse because of the marriage. This principle was the result of a *Quranic* reform (4:7) that gave the woman the right to own and manage property and to keep possession of this property even after her marriage.

Dower Rights

Another right granted to the woman as a result of *Quranic* prescription is her right to dower *(mahr)*, intended to safeguard her economic position after marriage. Dower is considered to be essential in every marriage contract. It may be defined as a payment that the wife is entitled to receive from the husband in consideration of the marriage. As the *Quran* specifies: "And give women their dowers as a free gift" (4:4). In pre-Islamic Arabia, *sadaq* represented the husband's gift to his wife, while *mahr* was paid to the bride's father. However, Islamic law made dower payable not to the bride's father, but only to the bride herself. Like the contract itself, this action also made the woman a party to the contract and so the marriage agreement could not be considered a sale.

Dower could also be used as a means for controlling the husband's power of divorce, because upon dissolution of the marriage he is required to pay the total amount of the dower at once. In cases where the wife is divorced before consummation of the marriage, she has the right to one-half of her agreed-upon dower or, in Hanafi law, if there is no agreed-upon dower, she is entitled to a gift of three articles of dress or their value. Such provisions are also derived from the *Quran:* "You incur no offense if you divorce women before the consummation of marriage or fixing the dower. And provide for them in the rightful way" (2:235), and "If, however, you divorce them before the consummation of marriage, but after fixing a dower, then [give them] half of the fixed dower" (2:236).

Dower may be classified into several categories. The first, specified dower *(al-mahr al-musamma)*, is usually fixed on the occasion of the marriage and recorded in a register by the *qadi* performing the ceremony. The amount of dower fixed by the father for his minor son binds the son for the amount; in Hanafi law, the father himself is not liable for payment.

Unspecified or proper dower *(mahr al-mithl)* refers to an amount that has not been fixed. Although it may not be specified, dower is a legal responsibility not dependent upon any contract between the parties. If dower is not determined, the amount will be decided by the social position of the bride's father's family as well as her own qualifications, such as those cited by the *Hedaya:* age, beauty, fortune, understanding, and virtue. The amounts of dower set for other females in the bride's family will also be a determinant. The husband's social or financial position is not a consideration.

The practice of dividing dower into two portions, prompt *(muqaddam)* and deferred *(muakhkhar)*, is universal in the Hanafi school. Prompt dower is payable upon conclusion of the marriage contract and deferred dower must be paid only on termination of the marriage and thus, as mentioned above, serves as a *bona fide* protection in the event of a divorce.

The wife's claim for the unpaid portion of her dower is legally considered an unsecured debt ranking equally with other unsecured debts due from her husband or, after his death, from his estate. The wife is entitled to receive the debt herself; if she predeceases her husband, her heirs, including the husband, are entitled to the dower.

Under Muslim law, a widow whose dower has not been paid is entitled to the "widow's right of retention," which enables her to retain (but not obtain) possession of her husband's estate until her debt is paid. However, her unpaid debt does not make her the owner of this property.

The guardian of a minor wife whose husband refuses to pay prompt dower may refuse to send the wife to her husband's house. In addition, before consummation, the wife may refuse conjugal rights until the dower is paid. Under these circumstances, the husband must maintain the wife, even if she lives outside of his house. However, the wife loses her right to refuse herself once consummation or cohabitation occur.

These elaborately developed laws for the husband's payment of the dower to his wife represent one part of his monetary obligations to the women in his family. In fact, this sum was often received by the bridegroom from his father or grandfather who, as the traditional head of the extended family, controlled all family wealth. In traditional times, not only payment of dower, but also the other extensive monetary obligations of the male for all his womenfolk, were collectively borne by the many male members of his close-knit family group, who often lived in the same household. Women in the family who were secluded, veiled, and restricted from most aspects of public life did not earn their own living. This role was traditionally reserved exclusively for the males, a role fulfilled as a point of honor. Women without an independent means of support were necessarily extensively protected through the legal maintenance obligations of their male kin.

Maintenance Rights

Maintenance *(nafaqah)*, another important obligation of the husband, includes food, clothing, and lodging. Maintenance is the husband's primary obligation, regardless of his wife's private means. The wife has priority over her children for maintenance. In return for her maintenance, the wife owes the husband her faithfulness and obedience. The husband's obligation begins when his wife reaches puberty and continues unless she refuses him conjugal rights or is otherwise disobedient. However, if her behavior is caused by nonpayment of prompt dower or the necessity of leaving her husband's house because of his cruelty, maintenance must still be paid.

A wife is also entitled to maintenance during the period of *iddah* following a divorce, and if she ceases to menstruate before the completion of this period, the wife is entitled to maintenance until she completes three menstrual cycles. This ruling is intended to protect women who may be pregnant. However, a widow does not receive maintenance during the *iddah* following her husband's death as maintenance is considered to be inconsistent with her position as an heir.

If the husband refuses to pay maintenance, the wife has the right to sue for it. The various schools of law have defined the extent of her rights in this situation in different ways. The Hanafi school shows more preference for the male in that it does not allow the wife the right to past maintenance unless a distinct agreement was previously made. The wife who, after a period of time, sues for maintenance, has no means to obtain payment of her husband's past-due debt. In contrast, the Shafii and Hanbali schools consider maintenance arrears to be the husband's ongoing debt that can be claimed regardless of the amount of time that has elapsed.

In classical Hanafi law, the wife is put at a further disadvantage economically by the fact that neither inability nor refusal to maintain is considered sufficient grounds for the dissolution of a marriage. This is contrary to the principles of both the Maliki and the Shafii schools. The hardships resulting from the traditional Hanafi position are numerous. For example, a wife, who in traditional society is unable to support herself and her children, is also unable to free herself from a husband who has been imprisoned for a number of years.

A father is also bound to maintain those of his children falling into the following categories:

1.   his infant children, regardless of whether he has custody of them;
2.   the infant children of a son who is unable to do so;
3.   his disabled son or student son;
4.   his unmarried daughter of any age; and
5.   his widowed or divorced daughter if she is ill.

If the father is poor, the mother and then the paternal grandfather are bound to maintain the children.[7]

Maintenance is not required of a father-in-law for a widowed daughter-in-law, and a father is not bound to maintain his illegitimate children.

The close ties between members of the larger family are reflected in the laws governing the maintenance of other relatives. Persons who are not poor are bound to maintain their poor relatives. The maintenance required should be determined in proportion to the share which they would inherit from these relatives at their death.

Parentage

Parentage is established in Islam by birth during a regular or irregular (but not a void) marriage, or by the father's acknowledgement. Thus, the child's rights to legitimacy are at times dependent upon the goodwill of his father. A child's legitimacy determines both his rights to maintenance and to inheritance from his father.

Legitimacy is determined in classical Islamic law by the following rules: (1) A child who is born within six months of a marriage is considered illegitimate unless the father acknowledges him. (2) A child who is born after six months of marriage is considered legitimate unless the father disclaims him. (3) After the dissolution of the marriage, a child is considered legitimate if born within two years (in Hanafi law).[8]

The father's acknowledgement of paternity *(iqrar)* is possible and effective under the following conditions: (1) when the father of a child is not known to be anyone else; (2) if the man could, at the time the child was conceived, have been the husband of the mother [this condition implies that it has not been provided that the child was conceived by illicit intercourse *(zina)* and that the alleged marriage has not been disproved]; (3) if the ages of the parties are appropriate for that of father and son; and (4) if the acknowledgement is not only of sonship but of legitimate sonship.[9]

Divorce

WHY DIVORCE?

Because marriage in Islam is the basis of society, the means by which the human race is perpetuated, it has always been viewed by Sunni Muslims as a permanent institution. Contrary to pre-Islamic practice, temporary marriages *(mutah)* are forbidden. The Prophet is reported to have said that "of all the permitted things, divorce is the most abominable with God." As will be seen, many verses in the *Quran* seek to limit both the frequency and the facility of divorce in pre-Islamic Arabia.

The negative attitudes toward divorce in Islam are clearly reflected in the opinions of Hanafi jurists. As the *Hedaya* states, divorce is "a dangerous and disapproved procedure as it dissolves marriage, an institution which involves many circumstances as well of a temporal as of a spiritual nature; nor is its propriety at all admitted, but on the ground of urgency of release from an unsuitable wife." [10]

However, consistent with its view of marriage as a contract, freely entered into by the two parties, provisions were made for legal action to protect the rights of each partner if the terms of the contract were not met. Every attempt should be made to maintain a marriage, but once the marriage becomes a failure, Muslim law allows the parties to separate from one another. Divorce in Islam serves as a safety valve in cases where the spouses can no longer live in harmony and so the very purpose of marriage would be defeated if they remained together.

DEFINITION OF DIVORCE

Divorce is generally referred to as *talaq*, meaning "repudiation." *Talaq* comes from the root *tallaqa*, meaning to release a human being from any obligation incumbent upon him. It signifies one spouse's release of the other spouse from the marriage bond, whether by repudiation or legal process.

As will be seen in the forthcoming discussion, the attitudes of the *Quran* regarding the necessary control of divorce are reflected in the approved forms *(ahsan* and *hasan)* of divorce. In comparison to the husband's unbridled right to divorce his wife for any or no reason at all with no further responsibility toward her in pre-Islamic Arabia, the forms of divorce approved and outlined in the *Quran* represented a significant improvement in the treatment of women. Nevertheless, although the *Quran* granted the wife some judicial relief from undesirable unions, the strong influence of social customs, especially in the Hanafi school of law, narrowly limited the grounds for that relief.

CLASSIFICATION OF DIVORCE

Divorce can be classified into five major categories: (1) *talaq* proper, (2) *talaq al-tafwid*, (3) *khul* and *mubaraah*, (4) *lian* and *faskh*, and (5) apostasy.

Talaq *Proper*

The first category and the most comprehensive, *talaq* proper, is the husband's right to divorce his wife by making a pronouncement that the marriage is dissolved. The male's extensive duties in the socioeconomic sphere, and the attendant dominant position of the husband in the family and society, are reflected in some of the consequent legal rights he enjoyed over his wife. That men were recognized as enjoying more extensive rights than women is most clearly illustrated in the Muslim male's essentially blanket right of divorce. Many *Quranic* verses make clear the undesirability of divorce and the punishments awaiting those who exceed the limits set by God.[11] However, the law did not translate these teachings and values of the *Quran* into specific legal restrictions on the husband's right to divorce to guard against abuses.

Conditional, contingent, or qualified pronouncements of divorce are permitted in Hanafi law. For example, a divorce may be pronounced to take place at the occurrence of some future event or at some future point in time.

The husband's pronouncement of divorce must indicate an intention to divorce, as for example, in the following expressions: "You are divorced," or "I have divorced you," or "I divorce my wife forever and render her *haram* (forbidden) for me." However, regardless of the verbal meaning, actual intention to divorce is not necessary. Because Hanafi law considers the action to be one of immense gravity, if the husband uses the formula of repudiation in jest, in drunkenness, or even under compulsion, it is still considered to be valid and effective.

Although it could cause hardships for wives of impetuous husbands, another consequence of this provision was that it provided wives of undesirable husbands with an unforseen opportunity to dissolve their marriages. In Turkey, for example, a convention developed during the rule of the sultans that allowed a wife to go before a *qadi* with two witnesses and claim that her husband had divorced her when he was drunk, a claim he would be unable to deny.[12]

A husband's act of divorce in Hanafi law is unencumbered. A Muslim who has attained puberty and is of sound mind has the right to divorce his wife whenever he wishes without citing a cause. The fact that the wife has no part in the procedure is further indicated by the fact that she does not have to be present nor must she be informed. The divorce can be either revocable, which gives the man an opportunity to reconsider the decision, or irrevocable. Because the Prophet did not approve of divorce, the revocable form of *talaq* is considered to be the "approved" form. Thus, the forms of *talaq* can be classified into *talaq al-sunnah,* divorce that is in consonance with the Prophet's teachings, and *talaq al-bidah,* divorce that does not follow the Prophet's teachings. The latter category of divorce represents an innovation and is therefore unapproved.

Talaq al-sunnah can be further divided into two categories. The first is *talaq al-ahsan,* the more proper and orthodox form of divorce and thus the least disapproved. *Talaq al-ahsan* takes place during the period of *tuhr* ("purity"—the time when a woman is not experiencing menstruation). If a woman is beyond the age of menstruation or if the parties have been separated for a long time, *tuhr* may be dispensed with. In an *ahsan* divorce, the husband utters a single pronouncement and then abstains from sexual intercourse with his wife during her *iddah.* The pronouncement is revocable (by words or conduct, as, for example, resumed cohabitation) during the whole period of *iddah.* This restriction provided a considerable period of time for the husband to reconsider his decision and for family arbitration to bring the couple together again, and thus followed the *Quran:* "Their husbands have the right in the meantime to take them back, should they seek reconciliation" (2:227). At the completion of the *iddah,* the divorce becomes irrevocable.

The *ahsan* divorce is the most approved form because of the kind and fair treatment given to the wife. Her period of suspense is not prolonged, and because there has been only one pronouncement of divorce there is no prohibition against remarriage of the parties. In addition, if the husband or wife dies during the period of *iddah,* the partner still inherits.

The *hasan* form of divorce is also approved, although to a lesser degree than the *ahsan* because it follows the letter but not the spirit of the Prophet's injunctions. The *hasan* divorce is carried out by making three consecutive pronouncements (the first two having been consecutively revoked) during three successive periods of *tuhr,* with no intercourse taking place during any of the three *tuhrs.* The first pronouncement should be made during a *tuhr*, the second during the next *tuhr*, and the third during the following *tuhr*. The third pronouncement serves as a final and irrevocable dissolution of the marriage, and with it intercourse becomes unlawful and *iddah* is required. Remarriage becomes impossible unless the wife marries another, consummates the marriage, and is then lawfully divorced.

The third pronouncement is irrevocable to prevent the practice of divorcing a wife and then taking her back several times in order to induce her to purchase her freedom by relinquishing her dower *(mahr)* or making some other financial sacrifice: "Divorce may be pronounced twice. Then they [women] are to be retained in a rightful manner or released with kindness. And it is unlawful for you [men] to take back anything of what you have given them" (2:228). Unlike the two approved forms of divorce, the two disapproved forms *(talaq al-bidah)* do not allow for a chance to reconsider a possible capricious or hastily made decision. These forms of divorce, similar to the husband's unfettered right of divorce in pre-Islamic Arabia, again made their way into common practice through the force of custom and were incorporated into Islamic law. They are valid but disapproved and considered sinful.

The first form of *talaq al-bidah*, consists of three declarations of divorce occurring at one time. The "triple declaration" is made during a single *tuhr* by pronouncing one sentence, "I divorce you thrice," or three separate sentences, "I divorce you; I divorce you; I divorce you," irrevocably dissolving the marriage.

The second version of the *talaq al-bidah* consists of one irrevocable declaration. The single pronouncement can be made in oral or written form during a *tuhr* or even at another time. At the moment of pronouncement or at the writing of the divorce, the marital tie is immediately severed.

The allowance of these two forms in law directly contradicts the *Quranic* prescription: "If you divorce your women, divorce them when they have completed their menstrual period. Calculate the period and fear God, your Lord . . . Those are the bounds of God. He who transgresses the bounds of God has surely wronged himself" (65:1). However, because Islamic law permitted the *talaq al-bidah*, only the husband's conscience served as a restraint from the use of such disapproved forms of divorce.[13]

Talaq al-Tafwid *(Delegated Divorce)*

In traditional Muslim law, while a husband enjoys an almost unilateral right to divorce, a wife's ability to divorce is very limited, a restriction that mirrors women's dependent role in society. It fails to reflect verses in the *Quran* that suggest a wider range of divorce options for the wife. For example: "And women have rights equal to what is incumbent upon them according to what is just" (2:227).

One power of the wife to divorce, strictly controlled by her husband, is *talaq al-tafwid* (delegated divorce), the second main category of divorce. Here, the power of divorce is delegated to a woman by her husband when he expresses such words as "choose" or "divorce yourself."

Khul *and* Mubaraah *(Mutual Divorce)*

A *khul* divorce comes about through the common consent of the wife and the husband: "And it is unlawful for you [men] to take back anything of what you have given them, unless both fear that they cannot comply with God's bounds. If you both fear that they cannot do that, then it is no offence if the woman ransoms herself" (2:228). This mutual consent includes the wife's giving some compensation (part or all of her dower) to her husband. However, awarding the dower is not absolutely necessary. A *khul* repudiation can also take place without payment of compensation by the wife. Indeed, the *Quran* explicitly forbids men from treating their wives unjustly and harshly in order to take back part of the dower, unless the women is guilty of open lewdness (4:19). The purpose of this passage is to set a limit on the man's attempt to push his wife into requesting a divorce.

Mutual divorce may take two forms: the above-mentioned *khul* if the desire to separate is expressed by the wife, or *mubaraah* when both husband and wife desire a separation. According to Hanafi law, the correct procedure for divorce involves one meeting during which the husband proposes dissolution and the wife accepts it. Once the offer is accepted, in both the *khul* and *mubaraah* divorces, it operates as a single irrevocable divorce.

Lian *and* Faskh *(Divorce by Judicial Process)*

Dissolution of marriage may also be brought about by judicial process. The first type in this category is *lian* (mutual oath swearing), where the husband alleges without legal proof that his wife has committed adultery. The wife then is entitled to file suit to bring about a retraction of her husband's statement or require him to swear an oath that she is guilty of adultery. His insistence upon her guilt under oath would bring the wrath of God upon him if he has accused her falsely. Once the wife has filed suit, intercourse with her husband becomes unlawful unless he retracts his claim. The swearing of the oaths in *lian* are governed by regulations in the *Quran:*

> And those who accuse their wives and have no witnesses except themselves, the testimony of one of them shall be to swear by God four times that he is truthful. The fifth time shall be God's curse on him, if he is a liar. And her swearing four times by God that he is a liar will ward off punishment from her. And the fifth time will be that God's wrath be upon her, if he is truthful (24:6–9).

After the oaths of both husband and wife have been made, the husband can divorce his wife. If he refuses to do so and the parties have not agreed to forgive each other, the court must dissolve the marriage, an action that has the same effect as one irrevocable *talaq.*

A second form of divorce involving judicial process is known as *faskh,* judicial recision of a marriage contract. *Faskh* means "to annul" (a deed) or "to rescind" (a bargain). In family law, it refers to the power of the *qadi* to annul a marriage on the petition of the wife. The grounds that are available to women seeking divorce in the Hanafi school are both limited in number and difficult to prove. In contrast, as we have seen, the husband is required by law to cite no grounds whatsoever to validate his repudiation of his wife.

The schools of law differ considerably in the number and kinds of grounds available to women who wish to divorce. The Maliki school is the most liberal, followed by the Shafii and Hanbali schools. The Hanafi school provides the narrowest grounds. In Hanafi law, a court may dissolve a marriage only if: (1) the marriage is irregular; (2) a person who has the option to dissolve the marriage exercises it; (3) the parties are prohibited from marriage by fosterage; (4) the marriage was contracted by non-Muslims who subsequently adopt Islam, or vice versa; (5) a husband is unable to consummate the marriage; or (6) he is missing. In the latter case, the court can declare the marriage ended after a period of time, enabling it to presume that the wife is a widow (putative widowhood). However, the wife must wait for a divorce for a period of ninety years from the date of her husband's birth.

In contrast to the Hanafi school, the more liberal Maliki school allows a wife to divorce on the grounds of her husband's (1) cruelty; (2) refusal or inability to maintain her; (3) desertion; or (4) serious disease or ailment that would make a continuance of the marriage harmful to the wife. As will be seen in Chapter 3, modern reform legislation looked to Maliki law to expand a wife's grounds for divorce.

Divorce by Apostasy or Conversion

In the Hanafi school, a husband's and wife's renunciation of Islam (apostasy) dissolves the marital tie, *ipso facto,* whether or not the marriage was consummated. This condition provides a possible opportunity for wives to dissolve their marriage, and cases can be found in which wives claimed to have committed apostasy in order to free themselves from their husbands.[14]

CONSEQUENCES OF DIVORCE (RIGHTS AND OBLIGATIONS OF PARTNERS)

Following a divorce, certain rights and obligations of both parties come into effect.

Iddah

The wife's main obligation rests in her observance of *iddah* to ensure that if she is pregnant no question will occur regarding the paternity of her child and his right to inherit from his father. In addition, her observance of *iddah* provides a period during which a reconciliation may take place.

Dower

Considering the husband's unilateral right to divorce and the potential wrong to which the wife is exposed, *Quranic* verses cite many conditions granting the wife compensation once the divorce is carried out, and these were incorporated into the law. If the marriage was not consummated, the wife is entitled to a suitable gift, if the amount of dower had not been fixed, or one-half of the agreed-upon dower (2:236–37). If the marriage was consummated, the total amount of dower is due immediately.

Maintenance

During the period of her *iddah*, the wife is entitled to maintenance from her husband, and this right continues, if she is pregnant, until the birth of her child. Furthermore, if the divorced wife has a young child, she can nurse him for two years. During this period, the father must maintain both mother and child (2:233).

Inheritance

Spouses may inherit from each other if their divorce is revocable. However, rights of inheritance terminate in the case of an irrevocable divorce.

CUSTODY

In Hanafi law, the divorced mother has the right to the custody *(hadanah)* of her male child until he is seven years old and of her female child until puberty, set at age nine. During this time, however, the father, who is legally considered to be the children's natural guardian and maintainer, continues in his supervision of the children and he or his paternal relatives receive custody of sons and daughters at ages seven and nine, respectively.

The awarding of custody to the father is a consistent social reflection of the workings of a traditional, patriarchal, patrilocal family. The family emphasizes the paternal line of ancestry and makes the central residence the home of the paternal grandfather, where many women (aunts, grandmother) are available within the family to care for children. However, such laws do not allow much consideration for the children's now-divorced mother, whose roles of wife and mother, the main source of a woman's status in a traditional society, may be taken away from her even though she was given no choice in the divorce action. In addition, if she marries another man, custody of her children, regardless of age, is given to her first husband as long as he is an able and proper guardian. A woman loses custody of her child at any age if her behavior is immoral or if she provides poor care for the child.

The collective responsibility of extended family members for each other can be seen in the following assignment of relatives responsible for the child. Such a list illustrates the exact assignment of duties to each relative, paralleling the exact assignments of their own maintenance and inheritance rights.

In the absence of or disqualification of the mother, female relatives in the following order receive custody: (1) mother's mother h.h.s.; (2) father's mother h.h.s.; and (3) full sister or other female relatives, including aunts. In the default of female relations, the following male relatives obtain the right of custody: (1) father; (2) nearest paternal grandfather; (3) full brother; (4) consanguine brother; and (5) full brother's son and other paternal relations (in the order of the nearest male relative determined in the same order as that of inheritance).[15] However, no male relative may obtain custody of a female minor unless he is related within the prohibited degrees of consanguinity. If no qualified guardians exist, the court appoints a guardian for the minor.

RECONCILIATION AND REMARRIAGE

The rules governing the process of reconciliation and remarriage of the spouses reveal the *Quran's* emphasis upon the importance of marriage and the gravity of divorce. Regulations seek to encourage reconciliation and remarriage while at the same time discouraging the divorce which had made a remarriage necessary in the first place.

If reconciliation and remarriage are desired by a husband and wife after a divorce, the parties are subject to the following regulations. If the husband has made one or two declarations of divorce in the two approved forms *(talaq al-sunnah)* following *Quranic* prescriptions, a reconciliation—either a formal revocation of the repudiation *(talaq)* or resumption of conjugal life—can take place during the *iddah* period. Therefore, formal remarriage is not required. Every possible allowance is made after an approved divorce is carried out to rescind the divorce and quickly re-establish married life. However, when one or two declarations in the approved forms have been made and the *iddah* period has expired, a regular remarriage is necessary. In this situation, the gravity of divorce is emphasized by requiring a complete renewal of the marriage agreement.

When three declarations have occurred, the divorce is final and irrevocable. Reconciliation and remarriage are prohibited. A husband who has pronounced a triple repudiation can only remarry his ex-wife if she marries another and that marriage is terminated through the death of her spouse or through divorce.

The intent of these requirements, which originate in the *Quran* (2:229), is aimed at curtailing such pre-Islamic practices as perpetually divorcing a wife, pretending to take her back, and then divorcing her again in order to either convince her to relinquish her dower for her final freedom, or to prevent her from remarrying and seeking the protection of another husband. The damage to his pride that a husband in traditional society had to endure in order to remarry his wife after an irrevocable divorce was doubtless intended to serve as a strong deterrent against hastily conceived divorces.

Succession

WHY INHERITANCE?

The customary laws dealing with inheritance in pre-Islamic Arabia were designed to keep property within the individual tribe, thereby preserving its strength and power. Inheritance passed only to mature male (agnate) relatives who could also fight and defend their possessions. Male minors were totally excluded. Widows, who were regarded as part of the estate, and daughters, who would no longer belong to the family once they were married, were also barred from inheritance.

The inheritance provisions in the *Quran* modified this system in order to correct injustices. Islam brought a change in the social structure. Loyalty to the *ummah* transcended tribal allegiance, and greater emphasis was placed upon family ties between husband, wife, and children. The consequent shift in allegiance from the individual tribe to the individual family unit significantly raised the status of women in the society. This Islamic reform is mirrored in the rules of inheritance stipulated in the *Quran* that were superimposed upon certain unjust customary laws. The *Quran* granted rights of inheritance to the husband and the wife, to children, and to a number of close female relatives who had previously had no rights of succession at all. These new "*Quranic* heirs" received fixed proportions from the deceased's estate before the inheritance passed to the close male relatives. Generally speaking, female heirs were awarded a share equal to one-half that of their male counterparts, whose heavy maintenance responsibilities also cited in the *Quran* justified their larger share. However, in cases where the parents and the uterine brothers and sisters of the deceased are only entitled to a small share of inheritance, men and women share equally in the estate. In addition, no reference is made in the *Quran* to primogeniture. Thus, all sons, regardless of age, received an equal portion of inheritance.

The reforms introduced by the *Quran* did not replace the existing legal scheme. Instead, the customary laws and *Quranic* reforms were fused into a comprehensive and coherent legal structure by the efforts of jurists and the force of events. The system of inheritance that resulted represents a feat of juristic achievement. The Prophet is reported to have said that the laws of inheritance comprise "half the sum of *ilm* (true knowledge stemming from divine revelation)."

DEFINITION OF INHERITANCE

The system of inheritance is the science of duties or obligations *(ilm al-faraid)*, specifically, religious obligations. The reform of customary law through its modification by *Quranic* verses (Islamicization) will be seen in the explanation of classical laws of inheritance that follows. The outline arranging the structure of priority in inheritance demonstrates both the structure of the traditional extended family and the Islamic concept of social values. Furthermore, it illustrates the meticulous precision with which jurists formulated this elaborate legal system of succession.

CLASSIFICATION OF HEIRS

Hanafi jurists divide the heirs into seven categories. The first three are the principal classes.

Quranic *Heirs*

The first class is made up of the *Quranic* heirs *(ahl al-faraid)*, whose rights were established by divine revelation. The *Quranic* heirs have been called "sharers" because they receive a precise fractional share prescribed by the *Quran* (4:11–12, 176). Although these relatives, who are mostly women, inherit first, they take only a portion of the estate. The strong influence of customary law can be seen by the fact that the residue, usually the bulk of the inheritance, reverts back to the male agnates *(asabah)*.

A list of the twelve relations that make up the *Quranic* heirs follows. It includes a treatment of (1) the fraction of the estate that each class of heirs receives, singly or collectively; (2) those relatives who exclude certain other heirs from inheritance; and (3) the other key circumstances affecting inheritance. The shares mentioned for each heir refer to the net estate, the amount remaining after funeral expenses and other debts have been paid.

The first two *Quranic* heirs are heirs by "affinity," the *husband* and *wife*. These heirs always succeed. They do not exclude nor are they excluded by any other relative. If they exist, they reduce the residue that may be taken by the second class of relatives (agnates). The husband takes one-fourth of his wife's estate. If his wife has no living children or children of a son h.l.s. (agnatic heirs), he takes one-half.

The wife inherits one-eighth of her husband's estate if there are children or children of a son h.l.s., and one-fourth if there are no children. However, the wife's portion is a collective one. In the case of a polygamous union, the wives share the one-eighth or one-fourth equally. The remainder of the *Quranic* heirs (blood relations) are listed below:

The *father* receives one-sixth. However, when there are children of the deceased or of the deceased's son h.l.s., the father of the deceased is made an agnatic heir.

The *mother* receives one-sixth. However, if there are no children of the deceased, no children of the deceased's son h.l.s., or only one brother or one sister of the deceased, her share is increased to one-third of the whole estate. If the husband or wife and the father of the deceased are alive, she will receive one-third of the residue after deducting the husband's or the wife's share.

One *daughter* of the deceased is entitled to one-half of the estate and two or more daughters receive two-thirds. However, if the deceased has a son, the daughter(s) are made agnatic heirs.

The *paternal grandfather* is entirely excluded from inheritance by the father or nearer paternal grandfather of the deceased. However, if they are not living, he takes their place, receiving one-sixth of the estate, or if there are no children of the deceased or the deceased's son h.l.s., he becomes an agnatic heir.

The *maternal grandmother* is entirely excluded by the living mother of the deceased or nearer maternal or paternal grandmother. The *paternal grandmother* is excluded by the living mother or father of the deceased, a nearer maternal or paternal grandmother and a nearer paternal grandfather. However, when they are not excluded, they receive a share of one-sixth of the inheritance to be distributed to one or more collectively.

The *son's daughter* receives a share of one-half for one and two-thirds for two or more collectively. If only one daughter of the deceased exists or if only one higher son's daughter exists, her share is reduced to one-sixth. Finally, if an equal son's son exists, she is made an agnatic heir.

The *full sister* of the deceased is excluded from inheritance by the deceased's son or son h.l.s., father, and paternal grandfather. If these are not living, one sister receives one-half of the estate and two or more collectively receive two-thirds. However, if a full brother exists, the full sister is made an agnatic heir.

The *consanguine sister* is excluded from inheritance by a son h.l.s., father, paternal grandfather, full brother, or more than one full sister. Otherwise, her share is one-half for one sister and two-thirds collectively for two or more. When only one full sister exists, the consanguine sister's share is reduced to one-sixth and if a consanguine brother exists, the consanguine sister is made an agnatic heir.

The *uterine brother* and *uterine sister* are excluded by the child, child of a son h.l.s., father, or paternal grandfather of the deceased. If these do not exist, uterine brothers and sisters receive one-sixth singly and one-third for two or more collectively.[16]

Agnatic Heirs

Once the *Quranic* heirs have received their share, the remainder of the estate passes on to the Class 2 agnatic heirs *(asabah),* or male relations on the male line. The inheritance rights of the agnates derive from pre-Islamic customary law.

Class 2 heirs have often been referred to as "residuaries," because the residue of the estate (often the bulk of the inheritance) goes to them. Class 2 contains all of the male agnates, and due to *Quranic* reforms, four specific female agnates.

Agnatic heirs are formally classified by the *Sirajiyyah*[17] in the following way:

1. Males—The agnate in his own right *(asabah bi-nafsihi).* This group, the largest and most important, includes a limitless number of blood relatives, all male agnates who were the tribal heirs of pre-Islamic law—the son, son's son, father, brother, paternal uncle and his son, and so on.

2. Females—The agnate in the right of another *(asabah bi-ghayriha).* This section specifies four female agnates *when they coexist with male relatives of the same degree:* daughter (with son), son's daughter h.l.s. (with equal son's son h.l.s.), full sister (with full brother) and consanguine sister (with consanguine brother).

3. Females—The agnate with another *(asabah maa ghayriha).* These consist of two irregular cases of full and consanguine sisters when they coexist with daughters and there are no nearer heirs.[18]

Uterine Heirs

Following distribution to the *Quranic* and agnatic heirs, the inheritance that remains is distributed among the uterine heirs *(dhawu al-arham)*, often referred to as "distant kinsmen." Uterine heirs include every relative who is neither a sharer nor a residuary. On close examination, one finds that the agnatic and the uterine together include all possible blood relatives of the deceased.

Following the first three principal categories of heirs described above, four subsidiary classes of heirs (successors unrelated by blood) inherit only as a rare exception.

Successor by Contract

In Hanafi law, in default of all blood relations and subject to the rights of husband or wife, the estate of the deceased goes to the "successor by contract." Through a contract, this person promises to pay a fine or ransom for which the deceased may become liable, and in exchange he receives this right of succession. Such an agreement is called a *mawalat.*

Acknowledged Kinsman

The next in succession is a person of unknown descent about whom the deceased has made an acknowledgement of kinship, not through himself but through another. The deceased could have acknowledged someone as his brother, the descendant of his father or his uncle, or the descendant of his grandfather, but not as his son.

Universal Legatee

The universal legatee is the person to whom the deceased, through a will, has left all of his property. The deceased may leave the whole estate if he has no living heir.

Escheat

In the default of all possible heirs mentioned above, the estate escheats to the government, the ultimate heir. In early Islamic history, the inheritance would go to the Public Treasury *(bayt al-mal)*.

TESTAMENTARY BEQUESTS *(wasiyyah)*

As the Hanafi inheritance laws so fully reveal, a man is not free to bequeath his whole estate to whomever he chooses. He is obligated by law to give certain fixed amounts to specific heirs. These shares represent the inviolate right of such heirs to an inheritance.

However, the verses of inheritance had been preceded by earlier verses permitting testamentary bequests to relatives. The law of testamentary bequests has its source in the *Quran:* "It is prescribed for you that when death is imminent for one of you and he leaves wealth, he should equitably make a testament in favor of the parents and the near of kin. This is incumbent upon the righteous" [19] (2:179). This *Quranic* "Verse of Bequests," which was of a general and discretionary nature, has generally been regarded by the majority of jurists as abrogated by the later *Quranic* verses of inheritance, which, as has been noted above, stipulated fixed portions for specified heirs. However, as will be seen in Chapter 3, a minority of jurists continued to maintain that the "Verse of Bequests" was in force. Modern Egyptian reforms have been based on this position.[20]

The *Quranic* verses of inheritance only provided for a specific group of heirs and this only "after payment of legacies and debts," so some form of bequest was still presumed (4:12). Because the *Quran* was silent as to the extent of this continued power of testamentary disposition, jurists turned to the *Sunnah* of the Prophet for regulations that both enabled bequests and protected the rights of *Quranic* heirs. The result is a system that recognizes the right of a Muslim to bequeath up to one-third of his net estate to parties of his own choice as long as they are not his own legal heirs. The bequest can be made for any person capable of owning property, regardless of his religion, or to an institution, or for a religious or charitable object.

The provision limiting the disposition of property to the "bequeathable third" is based on a report by the Companion of the Prophet, Saad b. Abi Waqqas:

> The Messenger of God visited me at Mecca . . . since I was near death. So I said to him: "My illness has become very serious. I have a good deal of property and my daughter is my only heir. Shall I give away all my property as alms?" He said: "No." I said: "Shall I bequeath two-thirds of my property as alms?" He said: "No." I asked: "Half?" He answered again: "No." Then he said: "Make a will for one-third and one-third is a great deal. It is better to leave your heirs rich than poor and begging from other people." [21]

The second restriction that a bequest may not be made in favor of a legal heir stems from the *hadith* reported by Ibn Abbas: "No legacy to an heir unless the other heirs agree." [22]

Sunni jurists devised a further regulation to cover cases in which a testator went beyond the limits of his power and bequeathed in excess of the allowable one-third or bequeathed to an heir. In such cases, the permission of the testator's heirs is required before such provisions can take effect. In Hanafi law, this consent must be obtained after the death of the testator.

Waqf (CHARITABLE ENDOWMENT)

The legal definition of *waqf*, or endowment, in the Hanafi schools is "the detention of a specific thing in the ownership of the *waqif*, or appropriator, and the devoting or appropriating of its profits or usufruct in charity on the poor or other good objects." [23]

The formation of *waqfs* is consistent with the strong emphasis on charitable deeds stressed in Islam, but in comparison with other institutions, its support in traditions is weak. The legal scholars *(fuqaha)*, in explaining *waqf*, put most emphasis on a tradition of Ibn Umar, which says that Umar asked the Prophet what he should do with valuable lands he had just acquired after the partition of Khaibar. The Prophet answered: "Retain the thing itself and devote its fruits to pious purposes." Umar followed these instructions, prohibiting the land from being sold, given away, or bequeathed, and giving it as charity to the poor, needy relatives, slaves, wanderers, guests, and for the propagation of the faith. In addition, the property's maintainer could also obtain sustenance from the property as long as he did not accumulate wealth from it.

Certain conditions must be met for the completion of a valid *waqf*. First, the *waqif* (founder of a *waqf*) must have reached puberty, be of sound mind, and be a free man. He must also possess unrestricted ownership and full right of disposal of his property. Second, the object of the endowment must be of a permanent nature and it must yield a usufruct (profit). A *waqf* is generally associated with real estate, although movable property has also been awarded. Third, the *waqf* must be made in perpetuity *(muabbad),* so that if it is established for individuals, the proceeds are allotted after their death to the poor. Fourth, the purpose of the *waqf* must be pleasing to God. In addition, the ultimate purpose of a *waqf* must be *qurbah* (i.e., for the benefit of the poor).

Two kinds of *waqf* can be distinguished: a religious or charitable endowment *(waqf khairi)* involving mosques, hospitals, bridges, etc., and family endowments *(waqf ahli* or *dhurri)* for children or grandchildren, as well as other relatives or other people.

Only in Hanafi law can the *waqif* himself also benefit from the *waqf* after the dedication. For the remainder of his life or for a shorter period of time, he can take the whole of the usufruct from the *waqf.*

Waqfs can be made for the rich and the poor alike, or for the rich and thereafter for the poor, or for the poor only. Thus, when a *waqf* is given in favor of the *waqif's* descendants, the trust is in their favor as long as a single descendant exists. When they cease to exist, the usufruct will go to the poor. Some limitation is placed on the amount of the *waqif's* estate dedicated in certain circumstances. If a *waqf* is made through a will or during death illness *(marad al-maut),* the testator cannot award more than one-third of his estate without the consent of his heirs.

Conclusion

The study of classical family law demonstrates the practical bent of Islam, from its earliest days, in applying the divine imperative. The comprehensiveness of the early Muslim jurists' efforts is attested to by the highly developed and detailed regulations governing every aspect of marriage, divorce, and succession. As we have seen, these regulations embodied both *Quranic* reforms and customary legal practices.

Quranic reforms corrected many injustices against women, introducing new rights and, in some cases, guaranteeing existing rights—the right to contract their own marriage, receive dower, retain possession and control of wealth, and receive maintenance and shares in inheritance. At the same time, however, family laws were formulated to meet a woman's needs in a society where her largely domestic, childbearing roles rendered her sheltered and dependent upon her father, her husband, and her close male relations. Thus, family law reflected women's dependent position, as can be seen in regulations concerning witnesses, option of puberty, initiation of divorce, and rights of maintenance and inheritance.

Because men had more independence, wider social contacts, and higher status in the world, their social position was translated into greater legal responsibilities (especially in maintenance regulations), as well as more extensive legal privileges proportionate to those responsibilities. The most notable examples of such rights and duties can be found in the areas of guardianship of marriage, extensive divorce rights, wider privileges of custody, and greater shares in inheritance.

In its attempts to meet the needs of a particular social milieu, Muslim family law reflected the social mores of the time—the traditional roles of men and women and the function of the extended family in a patriarchal society. This understanding of classical family law, which demonstrates the interrelatedness of law and society, provides a valuable perspective for modern legal reform. It can be argued generally that the duties and responsibilities of men and women in classical law remained virtually unchallenged up to the twentieth century because they paralleled the socially accepted roles of individuals and the function of the family in a social context that reflected the same patriarchal structure under which the original law was formulated. However, profound social forces in modern times have affected the status and roles of women and the family in Muslim societies. This process has been accompanied by reforms in Muslim family law that have sought to respond to, as well as to foster, social change.

Modern Muslim Family Law in Comparative Perspective

Legal Reform in Egypt

REFORM IN THE OTTOMAN EMPIRE

IN THE MIDDLE of the nineteenth century, reform in the Middle East was initiated in the Ottoman Empire, of which Egypt was a part, through the promulgation of commercial and penal codes.[1] These codes, both in form and substance, were largely derived from European codes as a result of increasingly close contact with the West (especially France and Great Britain) in the nineteenth century. In addition, secular *(Nizamiyyah)* courts were established to handle civil and criminal law, and so the jurisdiction of the *Shariah* courts was limited to the area of family law.

These legal reforms were at first followed by Egypt as an Ottoman province. Foreign legal influence continued to prevail after Egypt gained judicial and administrative independence in 1874, and so, from 1875 onward, the Egyptian government enacted civil and criminal codes modeled on French law.

Islamic law, however, remained central to family law. In 1875, Muhammad Qadri Pasha, under official government sponsorship, compiled a code based on the classical Hanafi school that included 647 articles concerning family inheritance.[2] Although the code was never officially adopted as legislation, as a compendium of classical law it served as the major reference for Egyptian *Shariah* courts, as well as for the courts of other Middle Eastern countries.

Despite substantial official legal change in the areas of civil and criminal law during the latter half of the nineteenth century, Muslim family law, which had been practiced through the centuries, remained unchanged. The fact that no major legislation in family law occurred until 1920 was consistent with the lack of social progress in Egypt.

EGYPTIAN REFORMERS

The ills of a medieval society in a modernizing world had been identified and criticized, and the seeds for legal reform in Egypt planted, by such important figures as Rifaah Badawi Rafi al-Tahtawi, Muhammad Abduh, and Qasim Amin, who attempted to provide a Muslim rationale for change. Tahtawi, the most significant figure of the first half of the nineteenth century, emphasized the necessity and legitimacy of adapting Islamic law to new social circumstances. He recommended using the principle of *takhayyur,* an accepted method of jurisprudence that permitted a Muslim in a specific situation to go outside his own school of law and follow the interpretation of one of the other Sunni schools. This suggestion was adopted and used extensively by later modernists.

It was left to the next generation and Muhammad Abduh, often called the "Father of Muslim Modernism," to grapple with the reality of change and to articulate an Islamic rationale for reform. Recognizing the discrepancy between *Quranic* reforms and women's social status in the nineteenth century, Abduh criticized the waywardness of Muslim society: "The Muslims have erred in the education and training of women, and in not teaching them about their rights; and we have failed to follow the guidance of our religion, becoming an argument against it." [3]

Abduh was especially critical of polygamy and its deleterious effect on family life. As will be shown, the *Quranic* argument that Abduh developed regarding polygamy was to be adopted by all modernist reformers. According to Abduh, polygamy had been permitted in the Prophet's time as a concession to the prevailing social conditions. *Quranic* texts (4:3 and 4:129) establish the norm that more than one wife was only permissible when equal justice and impartiality were guaranteed. Because this is a practical impossibility, Abduh concluded that the *Quranic* ideal must be monogamy. [4]

While Abduh remained principally concerned with theological and legal reform, his associate, Qasim Amin, developed the social dimension of the modernist movement by focusing on the plight of Muslim women as a cause for the deterioration of the family and society. Amin was especially critical of arranged marriages, the wife's lack of power to divorce, and the husband's unlimited rights of divorce, all of which he believed perpetuated the bondage of women.

Following Abduh, Amin re-emphasized the original *Quranic* intent that divorce be viewed as reprehensible, although permissible when necessitated by failure of the marriage and of attempts at arbitration. As a step toward providing some relief, he recommended that women have equal rights of divorce with men.[5]

Reactions to Amin's feminist books, *Tahrir al-Marah (The Emancipation of Women)* and *al-Marah al-Jadidah (The New Woman)* and to his ideas were swift and harshly critical. However, his writings became a source of inspiration to many feminists. Huda Shaarawi, leader of the feminist movement in Egypt a generation later, hailed him as "the hero of the feminist awakening and its founder."[6]

MODERN FAMILY LAW REFORM IN EGYPT

In the midst of this social ferment, initial legal efforts for reform of law were made first in the Ottoman Empire and later in Egypt itself. Reform in the twentieth century was slow to gain momentum both because of the stagnant social situation and the political problems caused by Western intervention and World War I. Significant reform legislation did not occur in Egypt until 1920. From that time on, however, Egyptian jurisprudence and legislation provided the impetus for modernist legislation throughout the Arab world.

Reform in family law occurred in the following areas: marriage, divorce, inheritance, and religious endowments.

Marriage

In 1897, the *Egyptian Code of Organization and Procedure for Shariah Courts* required written documentation in marriage, divorce, and certain inheritance claims. The traditional oral contract, through which evidence was limited to oral (and, thus, often hearsay) evidence, had presented many legal difficulties, particularly false claims of marriage and denial of valid marriages, problems which in an increasingly mobile society undermined the institution of marriage and the family.

The importance of documentation was further delineated in the *Code of 1909–1910* as amended in 1913, which decreed that after 1911 all legal claims must rely on "official certificates" or documents written and signed by the deceased.[7] This requirement of official documentation was also utilized in dealing with a more specific social problem—child marriage. In 1923, registrars of marriage were instructed not to conclude marriages or register and issue official certificates of marriage for brides under the age of sixteen and grooms under the age of eighteen. Eight years later, the *Law of the Organization and Procedure of Shariah Courts of 1931* consolidated the above provision with the regulation that, henceforth, courts were prohibited from hearing claims of disputed marriages unless these marriages could be established by an official certificate. In addition, the courts were prohibited from hearing any claims in cases where the bride and groom had not reached the minimum age at the time of the claim *(Article 99)*.

By refusing to register child marriages and by denying such marriages judicial relief, the reforms severely limited child marriages indirectly. Direct intervention—the declaring of child marriages as invalid—would have been considered an act of *ijtihad* (interpretation), making passage of the law virtually impossible. The indirect means was justified on the basis of the doctrine of *siyasah shariyyah (Shariah* rule), the right of a ruler to take administrative steps where necessary to ensure that laws adhered to the principles of the *Shariah*.

Divorce

As the *Quran's* primary legislative concern was the improvement of women's status through the establishment and protection of her rights, so too the main motivation behind modern Egyptian family law reform was the uplifting of women's position in society. Divorce was the area most in need of reform. Modern legislation sought first to establish grounds that would enable women to sue for judicial divorce, and second to limit a husband's exercise of repudiation *(talaq)*.

In the Hanafi school, the authoritative school for Egyptian *Shariah* courts, there are virtually no grounds upon which a wife can free herself from an undesirable marriage except for her husband's impotence [8] or by exercising the "option of puberty." [9] Of the four Sunni schools of law (Hanafi, Maliki, Shafii, Hanbali) the Hanafi school is the most rigidly formalistic, as it was more concerned with the development of a logical legal mechanism than with intention. In contrast to the other schools, especially the Maliki school, which was the most liberal in this regard, under Hanafi law, wives had to endure desertion and maltreatment with no recourse through divorce.

The first changes in the laws of divorce occurred in the Ottoman Empire in 1915 with the promulgation of two imperial edicts *(Iradah)* granting women the right to sue for divorce in cases of desertion or the existence of a husband's contagious disease making conjugal life dangerous (venereal disease, leprosy, etc.). More important, these edicts were followed in 1917 by the *Ottoman Law of Family Rights,* which constituted the first officially adopted codification of Muslim family law in the modern period. This law granted a woman the right to divorce her husband if he was unable to consummate the marriage, was missing, refused to pay her maintenance, was in prison, suffered from venereal disease, leprosy or another infectious disease, or went insane after the marriage. In addition, a wife could request a divorce if she feared bodily harm from her husband or there was continuous fighting at home. The court was then left to determine the legitimacy of her complaint. This law became the springboard for reforms in Muslim family law throughout the Middle East.

Egypt undertook a similar approach in *Law No. 25 of 1920* and *Law No. 25 of 1929.* This reform legislation recognized four situations in which a woman could sue for divorce: (1) her husband's failure to provide maintenance *(nafaqah)*; (2) dangerous or contagious disease of the husband; (3) desertion; and (4) maltreatment. The juristic basis for this change was the doctrine of *takhayyur,* or "selection," as suggested by Tahtawi. Legislators were thus able to depart from Hanafi law and adopt the more liberal and equitable teaching of the Maliki school.

Islamic law had granted every wife the right to support or maintenance. However, the prevailing Hanafi opinion had caused great inequity, because the husband's responsibility for maintenance only specified present maintenance. He was not held accountable for past-due maintenance he had failed to provide unless a specific agreement dealing with such maintenance was previously made.[10] Thus, even in the most extreme cases of nonsupport, a wife lacked the right to sue for divorce. Prior to the passing of reform legislation, the maximum punitive measure for failure to pay maintenance was imprisonment.

To remedy this situation, *Article 1* of the *Law of 1920* decreed that maintenance was a cumulative debt owed by the husband to his wife, commencing with the first time the husband failed to support her.[11] The situation of a divorced wife was declared to be similar; *Article 2* stipulated her maintenance debt should be computed from the date of her divorce.

In nonsupport cases, *Articles 4–5* decreed that a wife could obtain a decree of maintenance that could then be executed from any of her husband's property. This stipulation differed from classical Hanafi law, in which maintenance could only be executed out of property similar in nature to the required maintenance (i.e., clothes, furniture, food, money, etc.).

However, the most significant legal innovation occurred in *Article 4*, which decreed that nonsupport resulting from a husband's incapacity or unwillingness to provide support constitutes grounds for a wife's divorce suit. The only exception permitted involves cases of destitution, in which the husband is granted a grace period of not more than one month.

If the husband is absent or imprisoned and if there is a lack of property from which his wife's maintenance can be extracted, the wife is then also entitled to a divorce on grounds of non-support. If, on the other hand, the husband is at a great distance or if his location is unknown, the wife is granted a divorce at once *(Article 5)*.

The key factor in maintenance cases is the willingness and capacity of the husband to support his wife. *Article 6*, while asserting the husband's responsibility to pay maintenance, provides him with a further period to prove himself—the *iddah* (waiting period). A judicial divorce granted in nonsupport cases is revocable, and payment of the current maintenance is proof of goodwill and sufficient to revoke the divorce. However, in contrast to Hanafi law, the husband remains responsible for past-due maintenance as a debt owed to his wife.

Although most of the modern reforms in Muslim family law were motivated by desires to better the lot of women, certain safeguards were also introduced to protect the husband from legal abuses with respect to maintenance and the maximum length of *iddah*. Hanafi law stipulated that should a woman cease to menstruate before the end of her *iddah* she was to receive maintenance until the completion of three menses *(quru)* or until she reached menopause, whichever came first. Such measures were intended to provide for the continued maintenance of a woman who possibly could be pregnant. However, because verification of the completion of three menses relied on the woman's testimony alone, abuse was possible, and, in fact, some women did claim maintenance for very extended periods of time.

The reform of this situation was achieved in two phases—the first in 1920 and the second in 1929. Using *takhayyur* and following Maliki law again, *Article 3* of *Law No. 25 of 1920* stated that *iddah* for maintenance ended if after nursing her infant (usually for a period of two years) the woman did not have a menses for a complete year (twelve consecutive months). The effect was to fix both minimum and maximum limits in cases where pregnancy was possible. Even if a woman were to lie about completing three menses, the fixing of a twelve-month limit meant the maximum *iddah* possible was three years without nursing and five years with, instead of the previously indefinite duration.

The 1929 reform carried the rules of maintenance for wives observing *iddah* one step further. While the 1920 legislation had set minimum and maximum periods for the *iddah*, injustices were still possible because women could claim observance of *iddah* for a maximum of three to five years. Complaints of such injustices were cited as the cause for the new regulation. Based on modern medical expertise, the maximum length of *iddah* was set at one year from the date of divorce. This standard was applied in cases of maintenance, as well as inheritance and paternity.[12]

An area related to the question of maintenance is the custody *(hadanah)* of children.[13] Responding to complaints of mothers that their children were removed from their custody at too early an age (seven years for boys and nine years for girls), the *Law of 1929* decreed that when in the judgment of the court it seemed beneficial, the court would extend maternal custody of children to nine years for boys and eleven years for girls *(Article 7)*. In this instance, the court chose to stay within the Hanafi school, and therefore reforms were minimal. The jurists failed to consider the psychological hardship to the mother. The criterion of the Hanafi school was that the custody of children pass from the mother to the father when the boy no longer needed a woman's services and when the girl had reached the age of desire. In fact, the majority view had set these ages at seven and nine, respectively, but the court chose to follow the minority of jurists who preferred nine and eleven.

The third and fourth grounds upon which a woman had the right to sue for divorce, maltreatment and desertion, were established through *Law No. 25 of 1929*. Maltreatment, or cruelty *(darar)*, finds its only support as a ground for divorce in the Maliki school.[14] Following this source, *Article 6* decreed that where a wife's allegation of maltreatment detrimental to the continued marital relationship is substantiated and reconciliation seems impossible, the *qadi* shall grant the wife an irrevocable divorce.

Furthermore, the law granted the wife the right to re-petition the *qadi* if her first petition is denied on grounds of unsubstantiated evidence. In the event of a second rejection of her petition, the *qadi* is required to appoint two arbitrators for the partners. Following the *Quranic* injunction "And if you fear a breach between the two, then send forth an arbiter, one from his family, and another from hers" (4:35), each assigned arbitrator should represent one of the spouses. If this is not possible, men acquainted with the circumstances of the case should be appointed *(Article 7)*. Their task is a thorough investigation of the causes for the marital conflict and the submission of recommendations to the court for a reconciliation *(Article 8)*. If reconciliation proves impossible, and if responsibility for the conflict lies with the husband, with both spouses, or if the source of the conflict is unknown, the *qadi* is instructed to grant a single but irrevocable divorce.[15]

The above concerns for justice and possible reconciliation were further underscored by *Article 10* and *Article 11*. *Article 10* stipulates that should the report of the arbitrators indicate a deadlock, the *qadi* is to order them to make a fresh attempt. Should their renewed efforts prove fruitless, then other arbitrators are to be appointed. Finally, the court is to render its judgment in accordance with the recommendation of the arbitrators' report *(Article 11)*. Thus, through detailed procedures, every attempt is made to insure a just and equitable decision.

The fourth and final ground for divorce is desertion. Hanafi law was particularly rigid regarding desertion. The only relief available to a wife occurred if her husband was missing for a period of ninety years from the date of his birth.[16] This was believed to constitute a reasonable amount of time after which the husband might be presumed dead. After the expiration of this period, the court would declare his wife a putative widow.

In response to this problem, the legislation of 1929 decreed that if a husband is absent for one year or more without sufficient reason,[17] a wife has the right to sue for an irrevocable divorce on the grounds of injury resulting from his unwarranted absence. If the husband can be reached, the *qadi* must inform him of the pending suit. The husband's failure to return or make arrangements for his wife to join him results in a decree of divorce. If, on the other hand, contact with the husband proves impossible, the court must then grant the wife a divorce immediately *(Article 13)*. Moreover, a petition based on desertion may be initiated even if the husband has property from which the wife's maintenance can be obtained *(Article 12)*. Thus, the importance of conjugal life was upheld as central to the marriage contract and payment of support was not allowed to substitute for the husband's presence.

Article 14 of the *Law of 1929* addressed itself to the husband's imprisonment, a specific kind of desertion that had been the source of much hardship. In an increasingly modernized society in which virtually all punishment for crimes resulted in imprisonment, the plight of convicts' wives, who were unable to free themselves from marriages that were financially and psychologically undesirable, became a controversial issue in the press. As a remedy, the law decreed that a woman whose husband had been sentenced to not less than three years may, after a separation of at least one year, petition the court for divorce.

The second major reform of Muslim family law in Egypt was the limitation of the husband's unilateral power to divorce his wife at his own discretion, at any time, and for any reason. The *Quranic* injunctions regarding just and equitable treatment of wives had been morally but not legally binding. Hanafi law, with its emphasis on form rather than intention, further complicated and contributed to injustice, because a divorce uttered by the husband under compulsion, intoxication, or jest was held to be valid regardless of the intention of the husband.[18]

Reformers sought to limit and correct this situation in *Law No. 25 of 1929. Article 1* decreed that all formulae of divorce uttered under compulsion or in a state of intoxication were henceforth invalid. Metaphorical statements with ambiguous meanings were also declared to be invalid unless divorce was actually intended.[19] This emphasis on intention found its sources (and hence justification) in the Maliki and Shafii schools, rather than the Hanafi school.

From a juristic point of view, the more radical reforms occurred in *Article 2* and *Article 3,* because their contents lacked any basis in the official (predominant) views of the four Sunni schools. Instead, individual jurists such as Ibn Taymiyah were cited as sources. This extension of *takhayyur* to the selection of an individual jurist as the authoritative source for a reform represented a new expansion of the principle.

The main issue taken up in *Article 2* was conditional expressions of divorce pronounced by the husband either as a threat against his wife (or third party) or as an oath to reinforce a statement. Once again, the effect of such pronouncements was made contingent upon the husband's intention, and not the mere uttering of formulae. The law stipulates that all such conditional utterances effect a divorce only if the husband really intended to dissolve his marriage.

An even more significant departure from traditional practice was the decree that regardless of the number of times indicated by word or sign, a pronouncement of divorce shall only be considered as single and revocable *(Article 3).* Thus, the practice of *talaq al-bidah* (the three declarations of divorce given at one time) which, although frowned upon, had nevertheless been recognized as valid by classical law, was finally rendered ineffective.[20]

The *talaq al-bidah* had resulted in many abuses of *Quranic* regulations. First, it bypassed the waiting period *(iddah)*, which the *Quran* had intended as an opportunity for reconciliation. Furthermore, because this divorce was irrevocable, remarriage was impossible without an intervening marriage of the wife to another man. One result was the practice of *tahlil* (making lawful), which aimed to circumvent the impediment to remarriage resulting from a triple repudiation. The former (divorced) husband would arrange the marriage of his former wife to another man *(muhallil)* with the understanding that upon consummation (real or pretended) the second man would then divorce her. Only then would the former husband and wife be free to remarry.[21]

The reforms of 1920 and 1929 did not include all the areas in the laws of marriage and divorce recognized to be in need of reform. In 1926, the Egyptian government appointed a committee to recommend reforms in Islamic law governing marriage and divorce. Influenced by the reformist spirit of Muhammad Abduh, the committee included three suggestions in the draft articles it submitted. First, (following Hanbali teaching) wives should be permitted to include stipulations in their marriage contracts provided that they were not contrary to the purposes of marriage. For example, a marriage contract might include a provision that the husband may not marry a second wife. Second, a man should be restricted from taking a second wife and officials should be prohibited from registering such a marriage contract without permission of the local *qadi*. Third, the *qadi* should be required to investigate petitions for a second marriage to determine whether the man was capable of equal treatment and support of a second wife in addition to his present wife and family.

The *Explanatory Memorandum* that accompanied the draft articles is especially instructive, for it contained not only juristic bases for the reforms, but also references to the contemporary Egyptian social situation to justify its suggestions. Regarding the inclusion of stipulations in a marriage contract, the *Memorandum* noted that oral promises are often made by prospective husbands but ignored after the marriage, a situation that leaves wives without written legal evidence through which they can cite their grievances and seek judicial relief. The argument for the draft articles concerned with restrictions on polygamy noted that the vast majority of neglected children in Egypt were the result of polygamous marriages contracted by men who were incapable of supporting even one family. Although the Egyptian Cabinet approved the draft articles, they caused such a controversy that King Fuad refused to support the proposals. As a result, they were not incorporated in *Law No. 25 of 1929*.

Similar recommendations were proposed by the Ministry of Social Affairs in 1943, 1945, and 1969. A major attempt at family law reform occurred again in 1971, when the drafting of a new constitution for Egypt raised the question of the role of the *Shariah* in the new constitution. Feminist leaders such as Dr. Latifah al-Zayatt and Fatimah Abd al-Hamid called for a "new law of personal status" that would address more effectively such major problems as polygamy, divorce, and custody of children.[22] Moreover, Dr. Aisha Ratib, a professor of law at Cairo University, called for the imposition of restrictions on polygamy and the requirement that divorce be obtained from a judge.[23] In November 1971, Ratib was named Minister of Social Affairs. The Committee for the Revision of Family Law (headed by Ratib) made the following suggestions: (1) raising the age at which marriage is legally possible to eighteen for females and 21 for males; (2) requiring permission of a judge for a polygamous marriage; (3) allowing divorces to take place only in the presence of a judge, who would first attempt a reconciliation between husband and wife (if a husband pronounces his wife divorced, although his act would be valid according to Islamic *Shariah*, he would be punished by law); (4) stipulating that the mother's guardianship of children be extended to the age of ten for boys and twelve for girls; or that her guardianship should last until "the coming of age" for boys and until marriage for girls; and that guardianship of children at any age should go to the most suitable of the parents;[24] (5) encouraging the "judge's specialization" to facilitate fair and competent handling of family law cases. (A number of judges exclusively concerned with "family law problems" would be provided so that each could devote sufficient time to study such cases and so that the judge could acquire a proper perspective in handling cases of divorce, alimony, etc. It was also suggested that cases involving family problems be handled by a female judge, who would be more capable of understanding the particular position of the wife or children in family disagreements.)

In addition, the committee recommended that special halls be provided so that each divorce would be discussed privately, thus guaranteeing "secrecy and safety" to the family involved. This would counteract the traditional argument opposing the handling of divorce cases in court because it would expose private family problems to public view.[25]

Law No. 44, enacted in June 1979 to further amend family law, was declared unconstitutional in May 1985 owing to procedural objections. Provisions in *Law No. 100 of 1985*, which replaced *Law No. 44 of 1979*, require that a wife be informed by registered letter with recorded delivery if her husband marries an additional wife, and grant her the right to sue for divorce if she claims moral or material harm from the additional marriage, regardless of whether or not this was stipulated in her marriage contract. This right is renewed every time the husband marries again. Furthermore, if the new wife was not aware that the husband was already married and subsequently discovers the marriage, she is also entitled to sue for divorce *(Article 11 bis)*.

Additional provisions in the law require the husband to obtain a notarized certificate of divorce, a copy of which must by given to the wife by the notary, informing her of the divorce, within thirty days. The terms of inheritance and financial rights, such as maintenance during the waiting period, become effective from the date of the wife's knowledge of the divorce *(Article 5 bis)*. A man who violates these obligations will receive a sentence of no less than six months in prison or a fine of no more than 200 Egyptian pounds or both *(Article 23 bis)*. These measures sought to remedy situations in which a man might repudiate, or claim to have repudiated, his wife without telling her, continue to live with her, but, at a later date, refuse maintenance for any children born during this period on the grounds of their illegitimacy. Furthermore, if a woman is divorced without her consent and without just cause, she is entitled to at least two years additional alimony in addition to maintenance during the *(iddah)* *(Article 18 bis)*.

As noted previously, Egyptian family law included a provision, known as *bayt al-taah* (house of obedience), that permitted a husband to restrict his wife to their home. Under traditional Egyptian law, a wife who "refused to obey" and left her husband might be forcibly returned by the police and confined until she became more obedient. *Law No. 100 of 1985* instead requires the husband to send his wife a summons to return home via an official. The wife then has thirty days to object in court and present her lawful grounds for refusing to obey the summons. If it becomes apparent to the court that reconciliation is not possible and the wife petitions for divorce, the court is to follow arbitration procedures *(Article 11 bis 2)*. Given the husband's unfettered unilateral right of divorce, this reform seems to be less for his protection than to free a wife from the constraints of *bayt al-taah* and provide her with a quick, effective means of divorce.

In the event of a divorce, a man must pay child support until his daughters are married or have enough money to support themselves and until his sons reach fifteen years of age or complete their education *(Article 18 bis 2)*. In addition, a divorced mother with custody of minor children may be awarded the matrimonial home by the court until she remarries or her custody of the children ends, unless her former husband provides another appropriate dwelling *(Article 18 bis 3)*.

Under a new law that came into effect in March 2000, a woman can divorce her husband, with or without his agreement, in exchange for returning to him any money or property he paid to her upon their marriage. This is a variation on *khul* divorce, with the major difference being that the husband's agreement is not required and the monetary reimbursement is limited to returning what the husband had given the woman upon their marriage, rather than allowing the husband to set the price of the woman's freedom. However, an amendment to the reform requires that the woman renounce the financial rights she would normally have in the case of divorce, namely maintenance during the waiting period and support for children in her custody.

The reforms further provide that the woman will be able to call upon the Egyptian government to garnishee her husband's wages if he fails or refuses to provide maintenance for her. In addition, if the husband disappears or cannot pay a court-ordered living allowance, the woman will have the right to draw money from a special state bank in order to provide for her family. These measures were passed with the specific purpose of redressing some of the abuses that existed in the divorce system as previously practiced, whereby the man had the unilateral and unquestioned right to divorce his wife, however arbitrarily, as well as the right to an infinite number of appeals with no time limit if a divorce is granted. Under the new law, the husband has the right to appeal the divorce during the ninety-day period following the declaration of divorce. Once that period has ended, the husband no longer has the right to appeal the divorce and the wife is free to remarry.

With regard to the Egyptian reforms, several points are noteworthy. First, as has been true in most Muslim countries, the penalties for noncompliance with the new law are relatively light—typically a short imprisonment or a light fine, or both. For example, a man who divorces his wife without adhering to the prescribed procedures is liable only to a maximum sentence of six months imprisonment or a maximum fine of 200 Egyptian pounds, or both. Second, noncompliance with the law does not render the action taken invalid. Thus, although a man is supposed to register his divorce of his wife, not registering it does not negate the action. This has led to concerns that actual practice has taken the teeth out of the law. Finally, it is ironic that Egypt, which was a leader in family law reform in the Middle East and continues to be a country in which women enjoy a relatively advanced status, still has not been able to pass legislation requiring that a husband obtain court permission for a polygamous marriage or a divorce.

SUMMARY

It is evident that the first Egyptian reforms in family law sought to improve the lot of Muslim women. A major concern of the *Quran* was marriage and the family, especially the safeguarding of the rights of wives. Thus, to preclude abuses that had crept into Muslim practice, reforms in marriage and divorce were introduced.

To prevent false marriage claims and especially to control the social problem of ill-conceived child marriages, official documentation of marriage transactions was required and the minimum marriage ages were raised.

To counter Muslim men's abuse of their right of repudiation *(talaq)*, reforms were introduced that restricted their exercise of the right, expanded the grounds entitling women to a divorce, and improved women's custody and maintenance rights. Again, a return to the principles of the *Quran* is evident.

In addition to reforms in marriage and divorce, attention turned to other areas of family law that were also in need of reform: inheritance *(faraid,* the allotted portions), testamentary bequest *(wasiyyah),* and religious endowment *(waqf).*

Inheritance

Unlike the family law reforms of 1920 and 1929, which had been *ad hoc* in nature and thus rather piecemeal, legislation concerning inheritance and testamentary disposition was drafted in systematic codes. The result was the *Law of Inheritance of 1943* and the *Law of Testamentary Dispositions of 1946.*

The thrust of the reforms reflected, as did the reforms in marriage and divorce, a desire to strengthen the rights of nuclear family members and to rectify injustices resulting from the application of certain rules from medieval textbooks that reflected and suited the extended family of traditional Islamic society, but no longer adequately met the needs of the modern world.

A prime example of the inequity caused by the misapplication of some traditional laws in modern society concerns the inheritance rights of collaterals (brothers and sisters) of the deceased. Hanafi law reflected the traditional family whose wealth maintained all other members in a large extended household. Therefore, collaterals of the deceased were completely excluded from inheriting by their father's father (paternal grandfather). The real injustice of this situation arose when, according to law, the deceased's wealth, which the grandfather had inherited, passed on to the deceased's uncle upon the death of the grandfather. In effect, then, the brothers and sisters of the deceased were excluded from inheritance by their uncle.

In order to strengthen the rights of nuclear family members, *Article 22* of the *Law of 1943* decreed that brothers and sisters were to enjoy the right of succession to the deceased's estate along with the grandfather.

A second important change introduced by the *Law of 1943* concerned the legal presumptions that determined the inheritance rights of a fetus. Although the general rule in all the schools was that a child must be born alive to inherit, Hanafi law admitted an exception in the case of a child stillborn owing to an assault on a pregnant woman. All four Sunni schools had held that the stillborn child of such an assault was entitled to a compensatory sum *(ghirrah)* paid by the perpetrator and passing to the heirs of the child. However, unlike the other schools, the Hanafi school extended this rule and concluded that the stillborn child had a general right of inheritance that then was passed on to his heirs.

Article 2 departed from the official teaching of all four schools, maintaining that the stillborn has no right to property, not even that of *ghirrah*. Rather, *ghirrah* was redefined as a payment to the mother to which she alone is entitled as compensation for the assault and her loss.

The more important and complex legal reform concerned the determination of minimum and maximum periods of gestation. The vast majority of jurists had considered six months to be the minimum period of gestation for a married woman. Her child's right of inheritance, therefore, was contingent upon its birth within six months of her husband's death, on the grounds that a baby born after this period may well have been conceived after the husband's death.

Influenced by modern medical opinion and attempting to make the law reflect the normal course of nature, the *Law of Inheritance* extended the minimum limit to 270 days based on a Hanbali opinion. A child born to a married woman within 270 days from the death of her spouse was considered to be the legitimate heir of the deceased *(Article 43)*.

On the other hand, the maximum gestation period, which under Hanafi law was two years for a revocable divorce and indefinite for an irrevocable divorce, enabled a widow to claim paternity for a child born more than a year after her husband's death—a medical impossibility. The inheritance rights thus claimed by the illegitimate child violated the rights of the legitimate members of the nuclear family. *Article 43* decreed that a child was entitled to full inheritance rights if he is born within a maximum of 365 days of his mother's separation *(furqah)* or widowhood.

Testamentary Bequests

Even more significant from the viewpoint of social and legal change is the *Law of Testamentary Dispositions of 1946*. Its two major reforms are: the acceptance of the principle of "obligatory bequests" and the recognition of a Muslim's right to make bequests to whomever he wishes.

Whereas the majority of Muslim jurists have held that the "Verses of Inheritance" *(faraid* verses) completely abrogated the "Verse of Bequests" (2:180), a small number of jurists (among them al-Shafii) maintained that this contention was only true of legal heirs who, under the "Verses of Inheritance," were entitled to a fixed share of inheritance. He maintained that it was praiseworthy *(mandub)* to make bequests to close relatives who were not heirs. Another jurist, Ibn Hazm, considered such bequests (to relatives who did not qualify as legal heirs) to be obligatory. Furthermore, other early jurists held that should the deceased neglect this obligation, the court should make the obligatory bequest on his behalf.

Basing themselves on such traditional authorities, the reformers further specified which relatives were to be entitled to obligatory bequests.[26] The specific problem necessitating this legislation involved the plight of orphaned grandchildren. Under Islamic law and the principle of succession that the nearer in degree excludes the more remote, orphaned grandchildren had no legal claim to share in the estate of their deceased grandfather and obtain that portion which would normally be due their predeceased parent if he were alive. Reformers were reluctant to interfere with the law of succession because no basis could be found in traditional authority for such an action.

In order to correct this injustice, *Article 76* stated that if a grandfather failed to make a legacy to his orphaned grandchildren in the amount to which their predeceased parent would have been entitled by way of inheritance, the court shall execute such a bequest from the estate of the deceased grandfather, provided that it does not exceed the one-third limitation.[27] Furthermore, all such obligatory bequests are to take precedence over voluntary bequests *(Article 78)*.

Article 37 introduced a change of far-reaching social consequence and one that departed sharply from the classical texts. Following the Prophet's alleged statement, "No bequest in favor of an heir," the general rule of all four Sunni schools was that bequests were restricted to non-heirs. Bequests in favor of an heir required the ratification of the remaining heirs.

In a major departure from classical Hanafi law, however, the *Law of Testamentary Dispositions* decreed that a bequest to an heir not exceeding one-third of the estate is valid and effective regardless of the consent of the other heirs. A testator is now free to will up to one-third of his estate to heirs and non-heirs alike. Such a change makes the Islamic legal system more responsive to individual circumstances. Previously, relatives who were wealthy or poor, loving or hateful, had been treated alike.

One special problem remedied by allowing bequests to be awarded to heirs involved the widow who received a very inadequate share. Her maximum inheritance had amounted to one-fourth of the estate; however, if she had surviving children, her share was reduced to one-eighth, an amount she may have had to divide with other wives in the case of a polygamous union.

The motive behind this reform legislation, as with most of the family law reform, was the strengthening of the rights of nuclear family members, as opposed to those of agnates in the extended tribal family. For example, the legislation alleviated the unreasonable situation in which a man with a daughter and a distant agnate relative (whom he might not know or might actually dislike) would be forced to award the agnate one-half of his estate.

Religious Endowment (Waqf)

The last piece of major modernist reform legislation enacted by the Egyptian government during this period was the *Law of Rules Relevant to Waqf of 1946*. Like the *Law of Inheritance of 1943* and the *Law of Testamentary Dispositions of 1946*, this new legislation was the product of the Committee of Personal Status, which had been established in 1936. The change introduced by *Article 1* of the

Law of Waqf of 1946 developed from the *Egyptian Code of Organization and Procedure for Shariah Courts* discussed earlier in this chapter.[28] The 1897 law had introduced the requirement of documentation to avoid the difficulties that often arose with oral testimony. The scope of this law covered not only marriage, but *waqf* claims as well, stipulating that the creation of a *waqf* must be accompanied by a document of declaration *(ishhad)*. Reform had been introduced indirectly by forbidding judicial relief in cases where the document was lacking.[29]

Subsequently, *Article 1* of the *Law of Waqf of 1946* took the direct step of requiring that the creation, alteration, and revocation of a *waqf* must be declared before the *Shariah* courts and registered as well.

In addition, the *Law of Waqf of 1946* also touched upon more substantial concerns related to the family. The law itself was in no way comprehensive. Rather, the purpose of its sixty-two articles was to bring the law of *waqf* into line with those of inheritance and bequests and thus correct two major abuses that had occasioned widespread criticism: (1) the *waqf* system had immobilized considerable amounts of land, causing its withdrawal from agricultural and commercial use (especially industrial development); and (2) many had used the *waqf* system to bypass the laws of inheritance by excluding a particular heir or by including those not entitled to inherit. Women, especially daughters of the founder of a *waqf*, were victims of this circumvention as fathers attempted to avoid giving married daughters their fixed *Quranic* shares in order to preserve the integrity of the family estate.

A common practice employed to bypass women's inheritance rights was the inclusion of stipulations which, if not adhered to, voided the beneficiary's right to income from the *waqf*. For example, a father would specify that upon marriage, his daughter would lose her share. *Article 6* corrected this injustice by decreeing that a *waqf* that was joined with a condition restricting freedom as regards a marriage or place of residence was valid, but that the condition was null and void. Thus, conditions contrary to the spirit of the *Shariah* would no longer be enforced by the courts.

A major departure from the traditional law, under which all *waqfs* had been perpetual, was the declaration in *Article 5* that all family *waqfs* must be temporary, not extending to more than two generations (sixty years) or two series of beneficiaries. Even public *waqfs* under the new law (except for mosques and cemeteries, which are necessarily perpetual) may also be temporary. The temporary nature of *waqfs* was further established by *Article 11,* under which the founder of a *waqf* created subsequent to this law was given the right of revocation. The rigidity of the *waqf* system was eliminated.

The purpose of this regulation was also to limit the effects of circumvention of the laws of inheritance by the founder of a *waqf.* Under the traditional system of perpetual family *waqfs,* discrimination had affected not only the disinherited legal heir but also all descendants *in perpetuo* whose needs and merits were unknown to the founder.[30] Among the principal beneficiaries of this regulation were the descendants of disenfranchised daughters.

The termination of a temporary *waqf* had raised much controversy in Egypt. *Article 16,* which had prescribed that a temporary *waqf* would end upon the death of the beneficiaries or the expiration of a certain period of time, raised the question of what would happen to the property no longer subject to *waqf.* The predominant opinion of the Hanafi school stated that the ownership belonged to God. The reformers, however, looked to the other schools for a resolution. The Maliki school maintained that ownership remained with the founder, while the Hanbali school taught that ownership passed to the founder's beneficiaries. The resolution was not the product of one school, but rather of both. The Egyptian law applied the Maliki rule in cases where the founder was alive and the Hanbali rule when the founder was dead *(Article 17).*

The method used to provide authoritative support for this change is known as *talfiq* (patching together). *Talfiq* is a method by which the views of different schools or jurists are combined to form a single regulation.

Perhaps the most significant reforms in terms of the family occurred in *Articles 23–30,* which provided for "obligatory entitlements" for the immediate family. Paralleling *Article 37* of the *Law of Testamentary Dispositions, Article 23* of the new law extended the right of a property owner to create a *waqf* not exceeding one-third of his estate in favor of whomever he desires, heirs as well as non-heirs or a charity.

This provision, like its parallel in the *Law of Testamentary Dispositions*, enabled a man to make extra provision for the needs of a member or members of his immediate family, such as his wife and daughters. In addition to their rightful inheritance as heirs under the law of succession, the usufruct of up to one-third of the estate might be diverted from more distant agnatic residuaries to members of the immediate family. It should also be noted that this legislation concerns the rights of descendants, parents, and the spouse (or spouses) of the deceased, and not grandparents or collaterals. These articles reflect the shift from an emphasis on the extended family to the nuclear family and the individual. The obligation for more distant relatives, who became increasingly separated as a consequence of social mobility, is lessened in law.

Two further provisions ensured priority of the immediate family. First, the *Law of Waqf of 1946* stipulated that should the owner of property wish to endow all of his property, such a *waqf* must be in favor of such descendants as were alive at his death. Only if none of them was alive could he make a *waqf* to whomever he pleased. Second, *Article 24* decreed that in all *waqfs* that comprised more than one-third of the deceased founder's property, the descendants, parents, and spouse (or spouses) had a right to an entitlement. This obligatory entitlement amounted to the equivalent of the *(faraid)* under their *Quranic* rights of inheritance, regardless of whether they were named beneficiaries of the *waqf*. Furthermore, this entitlement devolved upon their deaths to their descendants.

The effect of *Articles 23–24* was to make two-thirds of the founder's estate subject to the rights of inheritance and to prevent the circumvention of these rights by a false use of *waqf*.

The general tendency of the *Egyptian Law of Waqf* to protect the rights of members of the nuclear family was further reinforced by *Articles 27–29*. *Article 27* asserted the right of a wife to stipulate in her *waqf* that her husband's entitlement ceases should he divorce her or take an additional wife.

Articles 28–29 sought to parallel the *Law of Testamentary Dispositions* in protecting the rights of orphaned grandchildren. The new law permitted the founder of a *waqf* to grant to the children of his predeceased son or daughter an entitlement in his *waqf* equivalent to the obligatory share rightfully due his deceased child under

Article 24 had the child been alive at his father's (the founder's) death.[31]

As a result of all the foregoing regulations, the intention of the *Egyptian Law of Waqf* to protect the rights of a founder's immediate family and to bring the law of *waqf* more into line with reforms in inheritance and testamentary bequest was accomplished. Consequently, *waqf* was prevented from circumventing the reforms introduced in succession and testamentary dispositions.

Despite the reforms, on September 14, 1952, shortly after the revolution, the Egyptian government abolished all family *waqfs*. *Waqf* property was distributed among the beneficiaries in shares proportionate to their entitlement under the *waqf*.

This radical departure from traditional Muslim law resulted from continued criticism of the *waqf* and the claim that the reform legislation did not significantly eradicate the economic and social injustices caused by its abuse and misapplication in contemporary Egyptian society.

A review of the reforms in inheritance, bequests, and *waqf* reveal two general aims: first, to protect the rights of *Quranic* heirs, and second, to strengthen the rights of members in the immediate family.

The original purpose of *Quranic* inheritance legislation had been to ensure the rights of heirs by establishing fixed shares to which they were absolutely entitled. Among the principal beneficiaries were wives and daughters of the deceased. Through the centuries, however, certain practices and abuses had arisen that compromised the rights of the *Quranic* heirs. Reform measures, following the *Quranic* intent, sought to assure the protection of heirs. Legislation was passed that permitted testamentary bequests of up to one-third of an estate to heirs as well as non-heirs. Furthermore, to prevent the circumvention of the rights of heirs through improper use of *waqf*, several regulations were introduced: first, all stipulations contrary to the spirit of the *Shariah* were null and void; second, in all *waqfs* exceeding one-third of the estate, *Quranic* heirs were entitled to the equivalent of their "fixed shares"; third, a *waqf* of all the founder's property had to go to descendants, parents, or spouse before any other relatives. Finally, to protect an heir and the heir's descendants against a *waqf* created for the improper purpose of disinheritance, *waqfs* ceased to be perpetual.

Strengthening the rights of the more immediate family over the more remote agnates in the extended family is the second general purpose of the reforms. Legislation was introduced to ensure the inheritance rights of collaterals (brothers and sisters) of the deceased and to prevent their exclusion from inheritance by an uncle. In addition, provision was made for the protection of orphaned grandchildren of the deceased. Following the spirit of the *Quranic* "Verse of Bequest," which encouraged provision for needy relatives, the law of "obligatory bequest" was enacted to guarantee orphaned grandchildren of the deceased a share equivalent to that portion which their deceased father would have inherited had he lived. A similar concern is evident in *waqf* legislation, which enabled a grandfather to create a *waqf* for his orphaned grandchild equivalent to the share due the grandchild's deceased parent.

In general, the desire to permit greater provision for members of the immediate family is also seen in the laws that allow testamentary bequests in favor of heirs and encourage *waqfs* in favor of descendants, parents, and the spouse (or spouses) of the founder.

Legal Reform in India-Pakistan

BEGINNINGS OF REFORM

In India-Pakistan, as in Egypt, Muslim reform was generated by an internal process within the Muslim community and the external stimulus of Western presence and criticism.

The year 1857 is a focal point for the history of Islam in India-Pakistan,[32] for it marked the *terminus ad quem* of the decline of the Mughal Empire. A veiled truth now became a clear reality. Although there had theoretically been a Mughal sultan, in fact the British had been the predominant economic and political power since the early part of the eighteenth century. In 1857, the last Muslim hope of casting off the yoke of British domination died with the failure of what the British called the "Sepoy Mutiny," or what Hindu and Muslim historians refer to as "the first War of Independence." The resultant condition of the Muslim community after this failure has been fittingly described by I. H. Qureshi as "the lowest depths of broken pride."[33]

Prior to 1857, the Muslims, who had constituted the ruling class, found it difficult to adjust to the changes introduced by the British—the substitution of English rather than Persian as the official language and the introduction of a Western educational system. The general reluctance of the Muslim community to avail themselves of new educational facilities resulted in their relative dissociation from the educational and technological changes occurring in India. For example, between 1835 and 1870, the ratio of Hindus (who had generally accepted British reforms) to Muslims in government service was seven to one.[34] Both their inferior status in society and the failure of their last attempts to free themselves from British domination brought the Muslim community to what Ahmad Khan described as a "state of utter ruin."[35]

Muslim Reformers

Just as religio-political concerns in eighteenth century India had produced the reformer Shah Wali Allah (1703–1763), the political crisis of the nineteenth century produced Sayyid Ahmad Khan (1817–1898). Responding to his people's plight, Ahmad Khan recognized the need for a revival of the Muslim community through modernization. Like his Egyptian counterpart, Muhammad Abduh, Ahmad Khan endeavored to show that there need not be a conflict between Islam and modern thought, that reason and religion were entirely compatible. Influenced by the rationalist tradition in Islam advocated earlier by reform thinkers such as Wali Allah, as well as by the Enlightenment in Europe, Ahmad Khan viewed Islam as the religion of reason and nature. Like Abduh, he wished to provide the Muslim community with a rationale for accepting and harnessing the strengths of modern science and technology: "Today we are, as before, in need of a modern *ilm al-kalam,* by which we should . . . show that they [modern sciences] are in conformity with the articles of Islamic faith."[36] To accomplish this, he employed an approach that was both theoretical and practical. On the theoretical level, claiming the right of *ijtihad* (individual interpretation), Ahmad Khan wrote prolifically, producing his own commentary on the *Quran,* as well as many writings on legal reform.[37] Like Tahtawi and Abduh in Egypt, he recognized the need for educational reform and devoted much time and energy to its practical implementation. He established a scientific society for the translation and introduction of works on modern Western sciences (1864) and, most important, founded the Anglo-Muhammadan Oriental College at Aligarh (1874), which was modeled on the British university system at Cambridge. The Muhammadan Anglo-Oriental Educational Conference, established in 1886, promoted Western education in Muslim India and advocated women's education.

Although Ahmad Khan had chiefly concerned himself with religious and general educational reform, one issue in the social realm, his position on polygamy, is especially significant. As did Muhammad Abduh, Ahmad Khan utilized *Quranic* verses (4:2–3, 128) to argue that the marriage ideal in Islam is monogamy, because man is incapable of living equally with more than one wife at one time.

However, it was Mumtaz Ali, a scholar of the Deoband Theological School who had become associated with Ahmad Khan, who championed the social aspect of reform in India-Pakistan. Ali's special concern for women's rights led to the publishing of the journal *Tahdhib al-nisa* through which he expressed his views. Mumtaz Ali asserted the need for equality of women with men in marriage and social customs. Like his Egyptian counterpart, Qasim Amin, he stressed the right of equal educational opportunities for women, which would make for better marriages between intellectually equal companions. Ali refuted the antifeminist exegesis of some classical scholars, maintaining that their interpretations reflected not the meaning of the *Quranic* text, but the customs and mores of the exegetes' own times. In language strikingly similar to that used by Qasim Amin, Ali denounced most of the marriages in Muslim India as loveless servitude endured by women whose inferior position was the result of their lack of education and subjection to marriage laws and customs that needed fundamental reform. He criticized child marriages and arranged marriages, asserting that marriage must be based on love and free choice. Ali also followed Ahmad Khan's position regarding polygamy as a tolerated institution that must in contemporary society give way to the *Quranic* ideal—monogamy.[38]

While Mumtaz Ali provided the modernist social critique for reform, Chiragh Ali, a close protégé of Ahmad Khan, spoke more directly to the need for reform of family law to implement needed social changes.

Chiragh Ali viewed Islam as distinct from any particular social system. Failure to recognize this had led Muslims in the past to identify their social system and its institutions with the *Quran,* and thus to regard them as ideal.[39]

The law books of the four Sunni schools reflect the social system of Muslim society during the period of their formation. However, because society had changed, Chiragh Ali argued, Muslim law also had to be updated to meet new social needs. Thus, the legal manuals of the schools were not immutable sources to be blindly imitated *(taqlid).* Viewing Muslim family law in the proper historical context, *Quranic* reforms regarding women's position in marriage, divorce, and inheritance vis-à-vis pre-Islamic practices could be seen as truly radical: "Islam . . . changed the attitude towards women to one of respect, kindness and courtesy. The Muslim law of inheritance, giving a woman exclusive right to her own property, compares favourably with the British law. Man's superiority is recognized by the *Quran* only in matters relating to his natural physical attributes."[40]

These *Quranic* intents and commands (the spirit and letter of its laws) were diverted through the ages by the classical jurists who, in areas such as polygamy and divorce, developed laws that reflected customary practices often at odds with the *Quran.* Ali believed that an overhauling of traditional Islamic law to eliminate anachronistic customary practices alien to the *Quran* was essential to the modernization of the Muslim community.[41]

Anglo-Muhammadan Law

The practice of traditional Muslim law in India-Pakistan in the early stages of British rule was unimpaired by foreign intervention. Although many changes came about in other areas, the judicial attitude of the British was characterized by noninterference with the prevailing legal system. Traditional Hanafi law, which had been authoritative under the Mughal dynasty, remained in force. Gradually, however, mere British presence changed to an assertion of British power, especially at the end of the eighteenth century, when the British East India Company became more involved in the political and legal life of the country in order to protect its own interests. Initial interference occurred with *Regulation II of 1772,* the reorganization of the court system by which English law was applied in the British Presidency towns. In general, however, Muslims and Hindus continued to be governed by their respective religious laws in all matters.

This situation continued until the latter half of the nineteenth century, when the application of Muslim law was narrowed even further by the enactment of the *India Penal Code* and the *Code of Criminal Procedure* in 1862. Moreover, portions of the civil code were also codified. As a result of such measures, Islamic law in the Indian subcontinent, as had happened in the Middle East, came to be restricted principally to the domain of family law.

In addition to legislation, the functioning of the courts themselves was of critical importance for legal reform in India-Pakistan. Because judges were either Englishmen, or Muslims trained in British law, British legal principles and concepts were often introduced when, because of language deficiencies, knowledge of traditional (Arabic) legal texts was lacking or when justice and equity seemed to necessitate a departure from traditional law. More important, the Indian courts, following the British practice, operated on a case-law system of legally binding precedents. This was a direct departure from Islamic legal practice, in which the judge was simply to apply the law. The changes in substantive law resulting from the use of such precedents, as well as the adoption of British juristic methods, led to a legal practice so influenced by the British that it has come to be called "Anglo-Muhammadan Law."

PRE-PARTITION MUSLIM FAMILY LAW REFORM

Paternity and Putative Widowhood

The first important changes in Muslim family law in the Indian subcontinent occurred with the passage of the *Indian Evidence Act of 1872,* which substantially reflected English law in its two areas of reform, establishing paternity and putative widowhood. These reforms, only implemented in Egypt sixty years later, were quite progressive. Regarding paternity, *Section 112* established a presumption of legitimacy for a child born during a valid marriage or within 280 days of its dissolution unless nonaccess is proved. However, children born after 280 days from the date of the divorce may be declared legitimate by the court on the basis of medical evidence or other substantiated evidence. Following English law, the new law decreed that a child born within days after the marriage is presumed to be the legitimate child and heir of the husband. This rule departed from the six-months maximum norm of the classical legal tradition, which was not reformed in Egypt until 1943.[42]

The second change in family law introduced by the *Indian Evidence Act of 1872* concerned the minimum time necessary for the court to declare putative widowhood. The caution of the Hanafi law, which required a period of ninety years from the husband's date of birth to elapse before declaring a missing husband legally dead, was deemed excessive and unjust. The act decreed that after a seven-year absence, if attempts to find the husband failed, the court may issue a decree of death and, in effect, declare putative widowhood.

Child Marriage

In the areas of marriage and divorce, additional reforms in family law did not occur until 1929, when the *Child Marriage Restraint Act* sought to limit child marriage, a social ill even more common in the Indian subcontinent than in Egypt.[43] Minimum marital ages of sixteen years for girls and eighteen years for boys were established. The Act provided penalties for any male over twenty-one years who marries a child and for the parent or guardian who promotes, permits, or fails to prevent such a child marriage.[44] Most important, the courts were empowered to issue an injunction against a child marriage on the basis of a substantiated complaint *(Section 12.1)*.

Despite the prohibition and penalties, child marriages still remained valid, although they were considered illicit. While an attempt was made to curb a social ill, as in Egypt, lawmakers avoided countering an established regulation, preferring discouragement of an abuse rather than its outlawing.

Wife's Right of Divorce

Years passed before additional family law reform was implemented. While Egypt had granted some relief to women through the reform of divorce regulations in 1920 and 1929, such legislation did not appear in the Indian subcontinent until *The Dissolution of Muslim Marriages Act* in 1939. Ostensibly, the act intended to "consolidate and clarify the provisions of Muslim Law relating to suits for dissolution of marriage by women . . . and to remove doubts as to the effect of the renunciation of Islam by a married Muslim woman on her marriage tie." [45] The real purpose of *The Dissolution of Muslim Marriages Act,* like that of comparable Egyptian legislation, was to introduce reforms that would improve the status of women and grant them some judicial relief by establishing additional grounds for divorce, most of which were not recognized by Hanafi law, the official law followed by the courts of the subcontinent:

> There is no provision in the Hanafi Code of Muslim Law enabling a married Muslim woman to obtain a decree from the Courts dissolving her marriage in case the husband neglects to maintain her, makes her life miserable by deserting or persistently maltreating her or certain other circumstances. The absence of such a provision has entailed unspeakable misery to innumerable Muslim women in British India. Legislation, then, became necessary in order to relieve the sufferings of countless Muslim women. [46]

Added to the two grounds recognized by the Hanafi school, viz. the husband's impotence and the option of puberty, were a husband's desertion, failure to maintain, failure to perform marital obligations, severe or chronic (physical or mental) defects, and cruelty or maltreatment towards his wife. In addition, the 1939 legislation, in a renewed attempt to limit the occurrence of child marriages, broadened one of the traditional grounds for divorce, the option of puberty. Originally, the option of puberty in Hanafi law governed all situations in which a minor was given in marriage by someone other than the father or grandfather. [47] The new legislation granted a female minor given in marriage by her father or grandfather before age fifteen [48] the right to repudiate the marriage any time before reaching eighteen years of age, provided the marriage was not consummated.[49]

In the establishment of new grounds for divorce, the India-Pakistan reforms proved less far-reaching than those of Egypt. For example, a wife could only claim desertion as grounds if her husband was a missing person. However, the reform did reduce the waiting period for a deserted wife's divorce from the traditional ninety years after a husband's birth to a simple requirement that the whereabouts of the husband not be known for a four-year period *(Section 2.1)*. By comparison, the earlier Egyptian reform of 1929 had granted the wife a divorce after one year of her husband's unwarranted absence.[50] Furthermore, no provision was made for divorce in cases of desertion owing to a husband's unwarranted absence and so the importance of the presence of the husband to preserve a marriage was not recognized.

Maintenance was another ground for divorce. *Section 2.11* decreed that nonsupport for a period of two years is sufficient grounds for a divorce suit. A grace period was provided, during which time if the husband could satisfy the court that he had resumed performing his conjugal duties the decree would be set aside *(Section 2.ix.b)*.

Again, while improving the lot of Muslim women in the subcontinent, the law fell short of the coverage provided by Egypt's *Law No. 25 of 1920*. Unlike that of Egypt and many other Middle Eastern countries, the law of India-Pakistan, in fact, penalized women by requiring them to suffer two years of nonsupport before they could file for divorce. Furthermore, maintenance was not recognized as a cumulative debt as it was in Egyptian law, and thus a husband who indicated a willingness to pay present maintenance was able to avoid both the divorce and the payment of the past-due maintenance.

Another difference is the issue of a husband's imprisonment. Egyptian reform treated imprisonment as a form of desertion and therefore allowed a divorce suit after a one-year absence (the minimum term for all desertion suits) in cases where the husband was serving a minimum sentence of three years. The India-Pakistan law treated this as an issue of maintenance, stipulating that a woman whose husband had received a final sentence for a minimum of seven years was entitled to an immediate divorce *(Section 2.iii)*.

While the minimum sentence requirement (seven years) was longer in India-Pakistan than in Egypt (three years), the Indian-Pakistani wife could obtain her divorce at once without the Egyptian one-year waiting period, thus gaining immediate relief.

Chronic defects (physical and mental) were also recognized as grounds for divorce. A woman was entitled to sue for divorce if her husband had been insane for two years or was suffering from leprosy or a virulent venereal disease.[51]

Finally, a major reform occurred with the inclusion of cruelty *(darar)* as grounds for divorce. Cruelty, as defined in the law, amounted to physical mistreatment or mental anguish. The six subclauses accompanying this regulation provided great breadth. A wife may obtain a divorce if her husband:

1. habitually assaults her or makes her life miserable by cruelty of conduct, even if such conduct does not amount to physical ill treatment;

2. associates with women of evil repute or leads an infamous life;

3. attempts to force her to lead an immoral life;

4. disposes of her property or prevents her from exercising her legal rights over it;

5. obstructs her in the observance of her religious profession or practice; or

6. has more wives than one and does not treat her with equality in accordance with the injunctions of the *Quran (Section 2.viii).*

This last subclause is the one instance in which the Indian-Pakistani reform followed Maliki rules more closely than the Egyptian reform legislation, which did not include the stipulation regarding equitable treatment.

However, although the reformers claimed to be substituting Maliki principles where Hanafi principles were found wanting, they completely omitted the rather detailed Maliki procedures for using arbitrators, which the Egyptian reforms included for all maltreatment cases.[52]

Besides differences in their substantive reforms, India-Pakistan and Egypt must also be contrasted in the method by which divorce is granted. *The Dissolution of Muslim Marriages Act* adopted judicial decree *(faskh)*, rather than Maliki law's judicial repudiation *(talaq),* which is used in Egypt's *Law No. 25 of 1929*. This difference has practical consequences. The *talaq* used by Egypt is a revocable repudiation that only becomes final at the end of the *iddah* period. *Faskh,* adopted by India-Pakistan, becomes final upon its issuance by the court. It is irrevocable and bypasses the *iddah* period with its provisions for reconciliation and maintenance.

Finally, a clear departure from traditional teaching occurs in the fourth section of India-Pakistan's law, which decreed that a Muslim woman's renunciation of Islam or conversion to a faith other than Islam shall not dissolve her marriage. This particular reform reflects the lot of women prior to this divorce legislation. Lacking sufficient means for relief from intolerable marital situations, some Muslim women were renouncing Islam or nominally claiming conversion to another faith in order to qualify under traditional Hanafi law for a dissolution of their marriage.

POST-PARTITION FAMILY LAW REFORMS

Reform Through Judicial Precedent

Despite the reforms rendered by *The Dissolution of Muslim Marriages Act,* inequity still remained, for there were many marital situations in which the wife could not fulfill all the requirements of the specific grounds recognized in the Act. Women entrapped by marriages in which incompatibility of the partners made the union an unjust hardship lacked the right to free themselves through divorce, a right that men had always enjoyed.

Traditional Hanafi law did not recognize incompatibility of temperaments as a legitimate ground for a wife to seek a *khul* divorce. This position was reaffirmed in 1952 by the Pakistan Supreme Court in *Sayeeda Khanam v. Muhammad Sami.*[53] In a full bench decision, the court observed: "If the wives were allowed to dissolve their marriage without consent of their husbands by merely giving up their dowers, paid or promised to be paid, the institution of marriage would be meaningless as there would be no stability attached to it."[54]

However, by 1959, this position was changed in *Balquis Fatima v. Najm-ul-Ikram Qureshi,* by the High Court of Lahore. The court asserted its right to grant a *khul* divorce where serious incompatibility made a harmonious marriage impossible. According to Hanafi law, a *khul* divorce was extrajudicial, based on mutual agreement and, most important, dependent upon the husband's consent for its validity.[55] However, basing themselves on the *Quranic* verse "Unless they both fear that they cannot comply with God's bounds . . . then it is no offence if the woman ransoms herself" (2:228), the court's interpretation was that the judge has the power to separate the spouses and so dissolve their marriage. Thus, the Lahore High Court, through its interpretation of Islamic sources, departed from traditional Hanafi law and allowed judicial dissolution of a marriage upon evidence that "the limits of God will not be observed, that is, in their relations to one another, the spouses will not obey God, that a harmonious married state as envisaged by Islam, will not be possible."[56] The requirements set for a wife seeking such a divorce were (1) showing that incompatibility prevented a harmonious marriage, and (2) returning her dower. The Maliki school had allowed a dissolution on similar grounds by arbitrators appointed to examine and resolve a case of serious marital discord either through reconciliation or, where this proved impossible, dissolution of the marriage. However, the High Court in no way followed or prescribed the detailed procedural steps prescribed by the Malikis.

That the court sought to remedy the social injustice suffered by women can be seen in the justices' observation that, "The marriage has to be terminated because it is not a reasonably possible view that a marriage must continue even though the husband misbehaves, or is unable to perform his obligation or for no fault of the wife it would be cruel to continue it."[57] This position of the High Court was given the highest approbation in 1967, when, in the case of *Khurshid Bibi v. Mohamed Amin,* the Supreme Court, the highest judicial authority in Pakistan, declared that Khurshid Bibi was entitled to a divorce upon returning her dower to her husband. Thus, while the right of the man to repudiate his wife has remained unfettered, the granting of a unilateral *khul* divorce to a woman in case of incompatibility represents significant headway in achieving a balance of rights.

Reforms in Muslim family law that occurred in the Indian subcontinent prior to 1947 continued in effect in both India and the new Muslim nation of Pakistan after the partition; legal reform in the new state also continued.

Reform Through Legislation

On August 4, 1955, eight years after Pakistan's founding, the Commission on Marriage and Family Laws was established to review Muslim family law to determine whether changes were necessary.

The commission was composed of three men, three women and one religious scholar (to represent the *ulama*). Their work resulted in the *Report of the Commission on Marriage and Family Laws of June, 1956*. The report represented the recommendations of the six laymen majority. However, shortly thereafter, in August 1956, Maulana Ihtisham-al-Haq, a religious scholar and a traditionalist, published a vigorous dissenting report taking issue with virtually every major recommendation of his colleagues on the commission. There subsequently ensued an extended debate between modernists and traditionalists.

In March 1961, many of the recommendations of the Commission on Marriage and Family Laws were embodied in the *Muslim Family Laws Ordinance of 1961*, which introduced reforms in marriage, polygamy, divorce, maintenance, and succession. However, the effect of conservative opposition to reforms can also be seen in certain provisions or qualifications that weakened the effect of the reforms and the omission of such areas as *waqf* reform.

MARRIAGE REGISTRATION. To avoid the difficulties of false claims resulting from oral contracts, Pakistan, like Egypt before it, introduced the requirement of written registration of marriages and created the office of *Nikah* (Marriage) Registrar to grant marriage licenses and oversee the registration of marriages *(Section 5.1–2)*. Failure to report marriages to the registrar became punishable by a fine or imprisonment, or both.

However, these restrictions were considerably weakened by the fact that failure to register a marriage did not affect the validity of the marriage and the maximum sentence for failure to register was only three months' imprisonment. The effectiveness of this law was further hampered because, in contrast to Egypt's *Law of 1931*,[58] judicial relief was not denied to unregistered marriages in Pakistan.

Thus, suits involving marriage, divorce, paternity, and inheritance in unregistered marriages were admissible in court.

POLYGAMY. Reform legislation was also introduced to limit polygamy. The law required the creation of an Arbitration Council, a new institution to handle polygamous marriage, divorce, and maintenance. A married man who wishes to contract another marriage is now required to obtain written permission from the council. Each applicant is required to state the reasons for the proposed marriage and the attitudes of his wife or wives toward giving their consent to the marriage *(Section 6.2)*. The chairman then organizes the Arbitration Council by asking the parties involved to nominate their representatives. Upon examination of the application, and if convinced that the proposed marriage is "necessary and just," permission is granted *(Section 6.3)*. In determining what is necessary and just, the *West Pakistan Rules Under the Muslim Family Laws Ordinance, 1961* suggests that the Council consider "Sterility, physical infirmity, physical unfitness for conjugal relations, willful avoidance of a decree for restitution of conjugal rights, or insanity on the part of the existing wife" *(Section 14)*. Decisions of the Council are subject to appeal *(Section 6.4)*.

A husband who fails to comply with the above regulations is penalized in the following ways: he must immediately repay the entire dower to his existing wife or wives; his wives have the right to immediate dissolution of their marriage;[59] and he can be imprisoned for up to one year or fined up to 5,000 rupees, or both *(Section 6.5.a-b)*. Furthermore, marriages contracted without the Council's permission are denied official registration and all cases which might arise from such a marriage are denied judicial relief *(Section 6.1)*. Despite these sanctions, all such marriages are nevertheless still valid.

DIVORCE. As previously noted, the *Dissolution of Muslim Marriages Act of 1939*, although supposedly following Maliki law, had in several important instances ignored Maliki doctrine concerning the grounds for divorce. Unlike similar Egyptian legislation, the Pakistan law has failed to include the detailed procedures for arbitration in cases where the wife sues for divorce on the basis of cruelty or maltreatment. This is especially noteworthy because the Maliki doctrine is based on a *Quranic* injunction (4:35).[60]

The 1961 ordinance remedied this deficiency by employing the Arbitration Council for all cases of divorce *(Section 8)*. To discourage hasty exercise of the husband's right of *talaq*, this reform legislation required written notice to the chairman as well as to the wife *(Section 7.1)*. A ninety-day waiting period is required during which the Arbitration Council will seek to reconcile the couple *(Section 7.4)*. The divorce does not take effect until the ninety-day period has elapsed or, if the wife is pregnant, until the completion of pregnancy *(Section 7.3 and 7.5)*.

Although failure to observe the above procedures is punishable by fine or imprisonment, or both, the penalties are relatively light (imprisonment of up to one year or a fine of up to 5,000 rupees) *(Section 7.2)*. This, coupled with the fact that failure to comply with the regulations regarding the Arbitration Council has no effect on the validity of the divorce, has diminished its effectiveness.

Paralleling an earlier Egyptian reform, Pakistan's reform legislation also decreed that all divorces are revocable, and thus remarriage without an intervening marriage is possible (unless this is the third such divorce). This reform returned to the *Quranic* law requiring three divorces, separated by a waiting period, before a divorce became irrevocable. As a result, it eliminated the abuse of *talaq al-bidah*, which had caused much social injustice by circumventing the *Quranic* waiting period. It also eliminated the need for both parties who had been divorced by *talaq al-bidah* to arrange for an intervening marriage before their remarriage was possible *(Section 7.6)*.

In the *Ordinance of 1961*, the Arbitration Council was employed in yet another area—a wife's claim of maintenance. The procedure involving the Council is similar to that used for polygamy and divorce cases. Prior to the passage of this law, several remedies were available to a wife who attempted to recover maintenance due her: application under Section 488 of the *Criminal Procedure Code*, a suit for recovery of maintenance, or, if two years had passed without maintenance, a suit for dissolution of the marriage. The new ordinance bestowed broad powers on the Council to review claims involving nonsupport or inadequate support and to award or refuse maintenance.

The All-Pakistan Women's Association continued to agitate for further reforms in marriage and divorce. The following were proposed as amendments to the *Ordinance of 1961*:

1. That in accordance with the *Quranic* sayings notice of the intention of divorce should be communicated to the Authorities before the actual divorce notice, so that there is a better chance of avoiding divorce. Also the wife should stay in her husband's home during her *iddat* so that by remaining together there may be some chance of their reconciliation.

2. The *Family Laws Ordinance* is silent on custody. The law should provide that whilst deciding about the custody of the children of broken homes, the court should keep in view not only the welfare of the children but also the wishes of such children.

3. That women who are divorced by their husbands without any reasonable cause or without their being at fault should be allowed reasonable maintenance by the husband as enjoyed [*sic.*] by the *Holy Quran.* "For divorced women maintenance should be provided on a reasonable scale. This is a duty on the righteous" (2:24).

4. Separate courts should be established (in which only family dispute cases should be tried) for family and marital disputes in all districts and cases be heard and decided by a special judge within a prescribed period of three months.[61]

Only the fourth proposal was acted upon. *The West Pakistan Family Courts Act, 1964,* established separate Family Courts "for the expeditious settlement and disposal of disputes relating to marriage and family affairs and for matters connected therewith."[62]

DOWER AND DOWRY. The other major significant family law reforms in Pakistan after 1964 and prior to 1979 concerned dower *(mahr)* and dowry *(jihaz).* While dower is a payment due to a wife from her husband at marriage, dowry is the obligation of the bride's family. In 1965, a High Court decision ruled that just as willful nonpayment of maintenance is grounds for divorce, so too willful nonpayment of dower is grounds for divorce.[63]

Dowry, although not rooted in Islamic law, is a firmly established custom. It consists of property such as clothing, money, and jewelry, which the bride's family is obligated to provide. Although the dowry theoretically belongs to the bride, it usually passes to the husband and his family upon marriage and, so, is often an important factor in arranging marriages. In the Indian subcontinent, dowry and lavish weddings have long been recognized as creating serious social problems, because family pride and a desire to provide a suitable marriage often result in the bride's family incurring substantial debts.[64] In 1967, the *West Pakistan Dowry (Prohibition on Display) Act* was enacted to alleviate this problem. The law affirms a woman's right as "absolute owner" of her dowry and bridal gifts, i.e., property given to the bride by the bridegroom or his parents *(Section 4.1)*. It also forbids the display of dowry and bridal gifts. However, the law did not address the more serious problems of excessive dowry demands by prospective husbands and lavish weddings. It was these concerns that led to passage of the *Dowry and Bridal Gifts (Restriction) Act* in 1976, which sought to regulate (1) dowry and bridal gifts; (2) presents, i.e., any property (other than dowry or bridal gifts) given to either spouse; and (3) wedding feasts. Its major stipulations included affirming the bride as sole owner of the dowry, bridal gifts and presents; limiting the total value of dowry, bridal gifts, and presents to 5,000 rupees *(Section 3.1)*; restricting the amount of money expended on wedding feasts to 2,500 rupees *(Section 6)*; and requiring that all dowry, bridal gifts, and presents be displayed *(Section 7)*, and that the bride and groom's parents submit lists of wedding expenses, dowry, bridal gifts, and presents to the Registrar of Marriage *(Sections 7–8)*.

SUCCESSION. The first law with respect to succession in the newly founded state of Pakistan was the *Muslim Personal Law of Shariat of 1948*, which legally and formally recognized a woman's right to inherit all forms of property. Elite Muslim women in Pakistan considered this law to be a first step toward women's empowerment through legal reforms and tried, although ultimately unsuccessfully, to use it as a justification for including a Charter of Women's Rights in the 1956 constitution.

From the juristic viewpoint, the most noteworthy reform in the *Muslim Family Laws Ordinance of 1961* concerned the law of succession. *Section 4* modified the traditional law of inheritance by introducing the principle of full representation for orphaned grandchildren of the deceased *(praepositus)*, that is, they are to receive "a share equivalent to the share that such son or daughter, as the case may be, would have received if alive" *(Section 4)*.

Although the Pakistani reform accomplished the same end as the Egyptian reform, the methods differed. Egyptian reformers, always more juristically conscious, avoided direct intervention in the law of succession; they chose instead to ensure the rights of orphaned grandchildren through the introduction of the principle of "obligatory bequests" in the *Law of Testamentary Dispositions of 1946*. Such a change had some juristic basis among traditional authorities. However, Pakistan's reformers, responding to the same social need, chose to meet this problem by legislating a reform in the law of succession, despite the lack of traditional authority.

The inheritance provisions of the *Muslim Family Laws Ordinance* ultimately met with severe criticism because of its failure to adhere to the Hanafi law of succession and to solve the social problems it was designed to alleviate. Religious scholars criticized the consideration of grandchildren as primary heirs to the exclusion of the brother of the deceased. However, despite criticism, the law has remained intact, although it was ruled applicable only to Pakistanis in *Federation of Pakistan v. Farishta*, PLD SC 120 (1981).

Compared to Egypt, Pakistan has not enacted particularly extensive reforms with respect to inheritance issues. Whereas Egyptian reform legislation has made possible a bequest to an heir of up to one-third of an estate, such legislation, which could potentially be beneficial to members of the immediate family, particularly wives and daughters, has not been passed in Pakistan. Furthermore, in the law of succession, where brothers and sisters of the deceased could be totally excluded from any inheritance by an uncle, their rights have been ensured in Egyptian law. Pakistan has no such legislation.

RELIGIOUS ENDOWMENT (WAQF). The history of *waqf* in India-Pakistan proves interesting both from the viewpoint of jurisprudence and the reform of substantive law.

As was mentioned earlier, the law of the subcontinent constitutes its own unique species—Anglo-Muhammadan Law. The normal procedure of the court in family law cases called for reference to authoritative texts of the Hanafi school in rendering decisions. However, under British influence, judges in practice also utilized the legal principle of equity. In cases where the bench decided that application of the letter of the law compromised equity, judges might choose not follow it. The exercise of this judicial independence led to a major legal crisis at the end of the nineteenth century in *Abul Fata Mahomed Ishak v. Russomoy Dhur Chowdhry*. The case concerned two brothers who created a family *waqf,* the income from which was to pass on to their children and then to their descendants until the family was extinct. Thereafter, the usufruct of the *waqf* was to be used for charitable purposes.

While the lower court initially confirmed the validity of this family *waqf,* the High Court in 1894 reversed the decision. On further appeal, the British Privy Council upheld the High Court's reversal.

The decision of the Judicial Committee of the Privy Council was based on the belief that such family *waqfs* provided no substantial gift to the poor. In fact, such a gift was illusory owing to its remoteness:

> It is . . . illusory to make a provision for the poor under which they are not entitled to receive a rupee till after the total extinction of a family; possibly not for hundreds of years . . . certainly not as long as there exists on the earth one of those objects whom the donor really cared to maintain in a high position. Their Lordships agree that the poor have been put into this settlement merely to give it a colour of piety, and so to legalize arrangements meant to serve for the aggrandizement of a family.[65]

In effect, then, the High Court had criticized the traditional law of *waqf* and rejected it in rendering a decision. Following the British legal principle of justice and equity, the justices had not simply interpreted and applied the authoritative texts (as is required under Islamic law), but rather had arrived at a new conclusion. Thus, the new criteria for judging the validity of a *waqf* would be a determination that the gift to charity was substantial and not merely nominal.

As might be expected, a storm of protest, led by such notables as Ameer Ali, the famous legal scholar and judge, arose from the Muslim community. Ali's work on Islamic law had often been cited by the courts in their decisions. However, in this case, the justices had rejected his defense of the *waqf* system. Despite protests, the decision of the Judicial Committee remained a binding legal precedent until the passage of the *Mussalman Waqf Validating Act, 1913.* This act, in effect, reversed the position of the High Court and the Judicial Committee and restored the Islamic law of family *waqf.* Addressing itself directly to the doubts regarding the validity of family *waqf* raised by judicial decisions, the law stated that "No such *waqf* [i.e., family *waqf*] shall be deemed to be invalid merely because the benefit reserved therein for the poor or other religious, pious or charitable purpose of a permanent nature is postponed until after the extinction of the family, children or descendants of the person creating the *waqf*." [66] Thus, through legislative intervention, the Muslim law of family *waqf* was restored. But the saga of *waqf* legislation continued even further. In 1922, in *Khajeh Solehman v. Salimullah Bahadur,* the Privy Council ruled that the *Waqf Act of 1913* had not been retroactive and, therefore, had no application to *waqfs* created prior to March 1913. Again, in order to override judicial legal interpretation, legislative recourse was taken in the passage of the *Waqf Validating Act XXXII of 1930,* which declared that the *Waqf Act of 1913* was retroactive to *waqfs* created prior to March 7, 1913.

Since partition, the only major legislation in Pakistan affecting *waqf* has been the *West Pakistan Land Reform Regulation of 1959.* Within this land reform legislation was a provision that declared that all lands not specifically dedicated for religious or charitable purposes shall cease to form part of a *waqf* (Para. 10.1–2). Otherwise, the law of *waqf* remains substantially unchanged. There has been no reform of the *waqf* system comparable to that of Egypt. The result is a system which often favors the extended family over the nuclear family. The *waqf* system in Pakistan, then, can still be used by the founder to circumvent the Muslim law of succession and exclude heirs, typically women. Furthermore, inequities resulting from such discrimination against female heirs will continue to affect the descendants generation after generation because a *waqf* is perpetual.

However, it should also be noted that the establishment of *waqf* has, at times, been used to protect female heirs over male heirs. The most important example to date was the Supreme Court decision in *Ghulam Shabbir v. Mst. Nur Begum,* PLD SC 75 (1977). This case centered on the creation of a *waqf* composed from seven-eighths of the property belonging to Haji Faiz Bakhsh. (The other one-eighth had previously been assigned to his wife and the mother of his son in lieu of a dower.) As custodian of the *waqf*, Haji Faiz Bakhsh named first himself and then his brother-in-law, excluding his son, Hussain. He and his descendants were to be the initial beneficiaries, holding the right to enjoy the income from the property and reside there. He also specifically stipulated that Hussain was to receive only 3 rupees a day from the property as his income and was to enjoy no other benefits from it.

Because Haji Faiz Bakhsh's only other nuclear family consisted of his wife and a daughter, it is clear that the *waqf* was set up to protect the women of the family after his death while excluding the son who normally would have had claim to the majority of the inheritance. After Haji Faiz Bakhsh's death, Hussain attempted to assert control over the property and even sold one-third of it on the basis of his claim to be the primary heir of the property and his assertion that the *waqf* was invalid because it overrode *Quranic* regulations on inheritance. The brother-in-law, as appointed custodian of the property, petitioned the court to determine whether a valid *waqf* had been declared. The court ultimately ruled in favor of the brother-in-law, commenting that the *waqf* could not be struck down on the basis that its object was the exclusion of someone who was profligate. Consequently, establishment of a *waqf* when used to circumvent Islamic inheritance laws can be used either to the favor or the detriment of women.

ISLAMIZATION. General Zia ul-Haq, who seized power in Pakistan by a *coup d'etat* in 1977, introduced an Islamization program in order to bring the Pakistani legal system into greater conformity with the *Quran* and Sunnah. Zia's program began with the establishment of a Federal Shariat Court through *Article 203 (C)* of the constitution. *Article 203 (D)* specified that the Shariat Court was to examine laws and legal provisions to verify their adherence to the precepts of Islam as laid down in the *Quran* and the *Sunnah* of the Prophet. If they did not conform, the court was then responsible for amending the law accordingly. Exempted from this requirement were the constitution itself and any laws relating to court or tribunal procedures. Constitutional changes were followed by Islamization measures—*The Hudood Ordinances of 1979*— outlawing *zina* (extramarital sexual relations), *qazf* (false accusations of unchastity), consumption of alcoholic beverages, and theft. The secular banking infrastructure was progressively replaced by interest-free banking for both Pakistani and foreign banks. In 1984, the *Qanun-e Shahadat Order of the Islamic Rules of Evidence Law* and *Ordinance XX*, often referred to as the *Anti-Islamic Activities of Qadiani Group, Lahori Group and Ahmadis (Prohibition and Punishment) Ordinance,* were introduced. Most important, in 1988, Zia introduced the *Enforcement of Shariah Ordinance,* which declared the *Shariah* as the supreme source of law and the guide for setting policy and making laws in Pakistan. A *Shariah* Bill and ninth amendment to the constitution requiring that all laws be in conformity with the *Shariah* were also proposed, but were protested by many organizations. Concerns ranged from claims that it would negate the principles of justice, democracy, and fundamental rights of citizens, to fears of sectarianism and divisions within the nation and the reversal of many of the rights women had already won under the *Muslim Family Laws Ordinance of 1961.* In April 1991, a compromise version of the *Shariah* Bill was promulgated, but the debate continues over whether civil or Islamic law should prevail.

Women activists were especially concerned by the *Hudood Ordinances* because of their discrimination against women. In particular, they cited the failure of the *Ordinances* to distinguish between adultery and rape, as well as the discrimination inherent in the rules of evidence established by the law. A man could only be convicted of having committed *zina* (adultery) if he had been observed by four other men in the act of penetration or confessed to the act throughout the trial. A woman could be convicted on the basis of her own medical report or pregnancy, which would serve as definitive evidence against her. A woman's own testimony about a rape has no testimonial value without the support of witnesses to the act. Consequently, a woman's charge of rape ironically often concludes with the victim herself being charged with *zina,* with a punishment of up to ten years imprisonment and thirty lashes for adults, and up to five years imprisonment and thirty lashes for minors. Fear of conviction for *zina* typically results in silence on the part of women, ultimately leaving rapists free to act as they please with no fear of punishment.

Women activists also protested the promulgation of the *Qanoon-I Shahadat* (Law of Evidence) in 1983–84, because it did not give equal weight to men's and women's legal testimony. Activists were concerned that women might be restricted from testifying in certain types of *hudud* cases (such as when they were the sole witness to their father's or husband's murder), and that their testimony in other matters would be irrelevant unless corroborated by that of another woman. Likewise, in 1984, women's groups launched a campaign protesting the promulgation of the proposed *Qiyas and Diyat (Retaliation and Blood Money) Ordinance,* because the amount of compensation to be given by the perpetrator of the crime to the victim or the victim's family for causing injury or death would differ depending on the victim's gender. Here, women activists were successful: the bill was finally passed in 1990 without the gender-discriminatory clause.

A case addressing the potential retroactive impact of the *Hudood Ordinances of 1979* sheds light on some of the legal arguments stimulated by the Islamization process. In 1982, the Federal Shariat Court heard the case of *Noor Khan v. Haq Nawaz* PLD FSC 265 (1982), a case that was based upon the alleged violation of Section 7 of the *Offence of Zina Ordinance of 1979.* Noor Khan alleged that the wife of his uncle had been forcibly kidnapped by another man ten years earlier. The complainant asserted that the man ought to have returned the woman to his uncle and that his failure to do so constituted *zina,* proof of which was the three children that the woman bore after the alleged kidnapping. The uncle claimed that he had never divorced the woman. As proof, he asserted that the chairman had never been notified of the divorce. The accused was ultimately acquitted by the additional sessions judge, who ruled that the Ordinance's requirement that the chairman be notified of the divorce by the husband was contrary to the injunctions of Islam, consequently rendering the law ineffective according to Article 227 of the constitution. However, the Federal Shariat Court responded by rejecting the judge's decision on the grounds that Article 230 of the constitution empowers the parliament alone to enact and change laws. Simply declaring a law un-Islamic does not automatically make it so or permit a judge to excuse parties from obedience to it. Furthermore, the Federal Shariat Court also rejected the charge that Section 7 of the Muslim Family Laws Ordinance of 1961 was un-Islamic. It is of interest that, although the initial judge's decision was rejected on the basis of its legal interpretation, the substance of the rendered decision remained in force, as the Federal Shariat Court decided that none of the parties involved was aware of the requirements of Section 7 of the Ordinance at the time of the divorce and that such a technicality was un-reasonably harsh against a husband and wife who had been living together without challenge for more than ten years. The legality of Section 7 of the ordinance was again raised in 1988, in the case of *Qamar Raza v. Tahira Begum*, PLD Kar 169 (1988), when the judge refused to recognize Section 7 on the basis of the notification re-quirement and the subsequent suspension of the effective date of the divorce until ninety days following such notification. Although some have argued that the existence of the law for twenty-five years with the acceptance of both religious scholars and lay people consti-tutes *ijma* of the community, the ordinance has not been enforced since 1988. However, it has been neither repealed nor abrogated.

SUMMARY

Laws were enacted in India-Pakistan to correct abuses in Muslim so-ciety by restricting child marriage and granting women the addi-tional Maliki grounds for divorce (failure to pay maintenance, desertion, and cruelty). However, the most significant piece of re-form legislation in post-partition Pakistan was the enactment of the *Muslim Family Laws Ordinance of 1961*. Besides abolishing the practice of *talaq al-bidah* and requiring the registration of mar-riages, reformers tackled three major areas of reform: the restriction of polygamy, the discouragement of hasty divorces, and the settle-ment of maintenance claims. This was accomplished by officially in-stituting a procedure recommended by the *Quran* for marital disputes (4:35). Arbitration Councils were established and, follow-ing the spirit of the *Quran*, were composed of representatives of the involved parties (husband and wife).

In addition, a direct change was effected in the law of inheri-tance to ensure the rights of orphaned grandchildren to their de-ceased father's share in his father's estate.

Finally, in a unique action in modern legal reform, the Muslim community, through its legislators, repealed the action of the Privy Council in abolishing *waqf* and reinstituted a long-established Mus-lim institution.

Legal Reforms: An Overview

MARRIAGE AND DIVORCE

Contemporary Muslim family law reform in Egypt and Pakistan reflects and reinforces several trends that have appeared in modern Muslim societies from Africa and the Middle East to the Indian subcontinent and Southeast Asia. Among the more significant are: a shift in emphasis from the extended to the nuclear family and emphasis on individual, rather than collective, identities and rights; a decreasing reliance upon informal channels of conflict resolution, such as intervention and arbitration by family members and community leaders, in favor of formal channels of conflict resolution, namely judges and courts; codification of the law; an emphasis on written documentation, rather than strictly oral testimony; and the expansion and protection of women's legal rights in marriage and divorce.

Analysis of contemporary trends in legal reforms concerning personal status issues reveals a willingness not only to increase public control over what were previously considered to be private matters between private individuals so as to work toward uniformity in the application and administration of the law throughout the countries in question, but also to address the question of social justice for women before the law by expanding and protecting their rights to actively participate in the processes of marriage and divorce. Women activists living in countries where Islamic law is upheld in matters of personal status note that the codification and unification of the legal codes and practices at the very least provides a legal guarantee of women's rights. It is the first step toward achieving and expanding rights. The second necessary step is educating women about the rights guaranteed to them by law and providing them with a supportive environment that encourages and enables them to pursue those rights.

Among the major changes from traditional law brought about by the codification and reform of the Islamic legal codes in different countries is a shift away from viewing marriage and divorce as private issues between the contracting parties to viewing them as matters of public order that must be registered and approved by legal bodies operating in official capacities. Indeed, countries as diverse as Algeria, Bangladesh, Iran, Iraq, Jordan, Kuwait, Lebanon, Libya, Malaysia, Morocco, Somalia, Syria, Tunisia, and Yemen require registration or notarization of marriages and divorces through either a judge or the courts. However, only Morocco requires a written contract in order for a marriage to be legally valid. Without a written contract as evidence, Moroccan courts will not hear any cases for divorce, maintenance, inheritance, paternity, or custody arising from the purported marriage. Other countries, including Jordan, Iraq, and Somalia, punish violations of the requirements with fines or prison sentences, or both, but do not invalidate the marriages.

Divorces are taken more seriously by the courts. Iraq, Kuwait, Libya, Malaysia, Morocco, and Yemen have specifically noted in their legal codes that only the court has the capacity to dissolve a marriage, rendering any divorce or repudiation declared outside of the courts invalid and anyone attempting to circumvent the law liable to a prison sentence or fine, or both. Malaysia further requires that the courts be advised of any revocation of the *talaq* in order for the revocation to be valid. Only Jordan and Kuwait allow a husband to actually declare the repudiation outside of the court, but require notification of both the court and the wife in order for the repudiation to become effective. Iran requires the registration of divorces, but this can occur only if the wife agrees to the divorce or the court grants permission for registration. Iran further curbs the husband's right to repudiate his wife at will by requiring any court hearing a divorce case to automatically refer the case to arbitration, in keeping with the *Quranic* ideal of allowing time for reconciliation between the spouses. A divorce is to be granted only if and when reconciliation proves to be impossible. Algeria, Malaysia, Somalia, and Tunisia also require an attempt at arbitration or reconciliation prior to granting a divorce, and in these instances the provisions apply regardless of which spouse petitions for divorce or the reasons behind the petition.

Modern legislation has implemented several legal provisions to guarantee the wife's financial rights. First, most legal codes absolutely guarantee the right of the wife to a dower upon marriage, because it is intended to protect her from destitution in the event of the husband's death or divorce. Indeed, Morocco, Syria, Tunisia and Yemen require the specification of the dower within the marriage contract in order for the contract to be valid. Bangladesh considers the dower to be a symbolic expression of the man's recognition of the economic consequences of marriage, so that lack of a dower would be understood as a man's unwillingness to fulfill his financial obligations toward his wife. Syria considers an unpaid dower to be a debt to the wife, second only to a debt of maintenance. The dower is the property of the wife and is hers to dispose of, invest, or manage as she wishes. For this reason, Jordanian law specifically states that the woman cannot be obliged to provide household requisites out of her dower. Libya, Morocco, and Tunisia further assert that the husband has no authority or guardianship over his wife's property or money.

In order to prevent anyone from trying to "sell" a bride in exchange for goods or money, Jordan, Lebanon, and Morocco prohibit the wife's parents or relatives from receiving cash or gifts from the prospective husband in exchange for surrendering the wife to him. Yemen expressly forbids stipulated conditions assigning the dower to anyone other than the bride. Only Jordan and Kuwait allow the father or paternal grandfather serving as marriage guardian to take possession of the dower, although Kuwait limits this right by permitting it only if the woman is less than twenty-five years old and does not expressly forbid the guardian to do so. Jordan does not require the woman's consent, even if she is of full legal capacity.

In some countries, dowers have become status symbols, engendering a competition of sorts between brides and their families to show which bride is "worth" the most. Consequently, countries such as Malaysia and Somalia have set upper and lower limits on the amounts of dowers permitted. In Malaysia, the amount of the dower differs by state—some states set the same amount for all women, while others vary the amounts according to the woman's social status.

In addition to the dower, the wife's right to maintenance is also guaranteed as an absolute right by most legal codes. In cases where the husband falls behind in paying maintenance to his wife, the wife has the right to petition the court for a ruling in her favor requiring the husband to pay the maintenance owed to her, typically dating from the time when he ceased to pay it, provided that not more than one year has elapsed since the last payment. The legal codes of Jordan, Kuwait, Lebanon, Syria, Tunisia, and Yemen specifically state that unpaid maintenance is a debt due to the wife that takes precedence over any other debt owed by the husband and that it cannot be cancelled by divorce, death, the passage of time, or procrastination on the part of the husband. Kuwait and Yemen further provide that maintenance cannot even be excused by mutual agreement. It must be paid.

The Malaysian example with respect to maintenance matters is quite useful in demonstrating how one country has tried to ensure practical application of the legal code. First, Malaysia requires as part of the marriage ceremony following the pronouncement of the contract an oath by the husband called *taklik*. *Taklik* is a promise made by the husband that he will provide his wife with maintenance. He proclaims that in the event of his failure to provide maintenance for six consecutive months, his wife may request intervention by the authorities. In cases where the court rules in the wife's favor, the *Islamic Family Law Act* grants the court the power to require that the maintenance be deducted by the husband's employer directly from his paycheck and turned over to his wife. Thus, in Malaysia, the court is granted the power to actually enforce its decisions, rather than just render them.

Tunisia and Somalia have reformed their laws regarding maintenance to reflect the modern reality of both husbands and wives working outside of the home and contributing to the support of the family: They require both the husband and the wife to participate financially in maintaining the household. Libya allows a husband to collect maintenance from his wife only in cases where he is in hardship and she is wealthy.

Most countries also guarantee the woman's right to petition for divorce if her husband does not pay her maintenance. The courts typically grant the husband a grace period, which can vary from between thirty days and six months, during which he is to prove his good faith by paying the maintenance owed. If he fails to do so, the court will grant the woman a divorce. Bangladesh requires the court to grant a divorce to any woman who has not been paid maintenance if she requests it. Some legal codes, such as Syria's, grant the husband the right to revoke the divorce only if he can prove his financial ability and willingness to pay maintenance. Other countries, like Kuwait, will grant a revocable divorce once. However, if the husband fails to pay maintenance a second time and the wife brings the case to the court again, the court will grant her an irrevocable divorce. In many cases, when the husband is experiencing financial hardships and is without funding or owes the wife a debt of maintenance, the court will grant the wife the right to incur debt for the purpose of maintenance costs in the name of the husband. Malaysia unequivocally grants the wife the right to divorce in cases where the husband is insolvent. Only Iraq specifies that the state will step in to support a wife in hardship who has no maintenance from her husband and who is unable to borrow from a family member or creditor. No such safety valve for destitute women exists in the other countries analyzed here.

Financial provisions have also been made with respect to divorced wives. Under classical law, a divorced wife is entitled to the unpaid portion of her dower and maintenance during her waiting period or during her custody over children under two years of age. Outside of this, classical law makes no provisions for financial support of a divorced wife. Many activists for women's rights in the twentieth century have questioned the fairness of a system that requires a wife to care for her husband, children, and the matrimonial home throughout the marriage, and then leaves her only three months' maintenance upon divorce, regardless of the circumstances surrounding the divorce, the wealth accumulated during the marriage, or the likelihood that the woman will fall into destitution.

Some countries have sought to redress such grievances by granting the wife the right to alimony. Syria was the first country to grant a woman who was divorced arbitrarily the right to compensation (up to three years' maintenance in addition to maintenance during the waiting period). Jordan, Kuwait, and Yemen followed suit, although the amount was limited to one year's maintenance in addition to maintenance during the waiting period. Algeria allows the judge to determine the amount the woman is to receive, which may include housing, based on the damages and harm she has suffered. Algerian law also grants the wife the right to collect damages in the case where the husband has abandoned the matrimonial home. Tunisia allows the judge to set the amount of compensation with the intent that it should allow the wife to maintain the same standard of living she enjoyed while married. Libya and the Ismaili Khojas of East Africa grant the wife the right to just and reasonable compensation whenever the divorce is the fault of the husband. Bangladesh does not allow the wife to be expelled from her place of residence or harassed by her husband. Expulsion and harassment are considered to be both criminal and moral offenses. Iraq and Malaysia grant the wife the right to the matrimonial home if the husband initiates the divorce in the absence of any fault on the part of the wife. In Malaysia, the wife retains her right to the matrimonial home until she either remarries or the husband is able to provide her with an alternative acceptable place to live. The husband is further required to give her a consolation gift *(mu'tah)*, which is usually money. Any man who fails to do so can be taken to court. Moroccan law also requires the husband to give his divorced wife a consolation gift to appease her for the harm she has suffered as a result of the divorce, regardless of who was at fault. Libya and Somalia grant the right of compensation to whichever party is determined to have been injured by the other in the case of divorce.

Thus, it is clear that modern legislation has moved both to protect existing financial rights for women under Islamic law and to expand them toward the goal of achieving social justice. Expansion of women's financial rights in this way is not done to oppose the *Quran*, but rather it is intended to supplement the minimum requirements outlined in the *Quran*. There is nothing in the *Quran* that forbids a man from providing more than the minimum legally required to his divorced wife. Indeed, the *Quran* repeatedly praises the practice of generosity and exhorts people to be fair and just in their dealings with others.

In addition to safeguarding women's financial rights, most Muslim countries have also sought to safeguard women's health and safety by curbing the practice of child marriage through legislation setting minimum ages for marriage. Post-revolutionary Iran presents some interesting insights into the debate between classical interpretations of the law and modern medical knowledge and reformist tendencies. Under the secular regime of the Shah, the minimum ages for marriage were raised to eighteen years for girls and twenty years for boys in 1975. The Khomeini regime changed the minimum ages back to those specified in classical Ithna 'Ashari law—nine years for girls and fifteen years for boys. However, upon recognition that sexual intercourse and pregnancy can be physically harmful and dangerous, if not lethal, to such young girls, the regime amended the law to raise the minimum age of marriage for girls to fifteen years. Furthermore, unlike other countries, there are no provisions in Iran for exceptions to the rule, regardless of who requests the exemption. This is enforced by punishing anyone who marries off a girl between the ages of thirteen and fifteen with a prison sentence of between six months and two years, which is raised to two to three years imprisonment if the girl is under the age of thirteen. The government further requires that the girl should have had her first menstrual period prior to her first marriage.

These initial steps toward reform have been accompanied by recent ongoing efforts by the Family Planning Board and the Ministry of Public Health to raise the minimum age for marriage for girls to eighteen years of age. Throughout the rest of the Muslim world, minimum marriage ages for girls range from as low as fifteen in Jordan, Kuwait, Morocco, and Yemen, to as high as twenty in Libya. For boys, minimum ages range from as low as fifteen in Yemen to as high as twenty-one in Algeria, Bangladesh, and Pakistan. However, these laws are tempered by additional legislation in Algeria, Iraq, Lebanon, Libya, Malaysia, Morocco, Somalia, Syria, and Tunisia that allows a judge to bypass the minimum age requirements in cases where the guardian agrees and there is some perceived benefit or necessity to the marriage. As a result, the absolute minimum age can be as low as nine and thirteen years of age for girls in Lebanon and Syria, respectively, and fifteen for boys in Syria and Iraq, provided that they are physically and mentally fit to fulfill the requirements of marriage. Only Yemen and Kuwait expressly forbid any exceptions to the minimum age requirements.

Modern legislation has also sought to protect and expand the rights of women as active participants in the contracting of their own marriages. Somalia and Tunisia are the most liberal in allowing both men and women to freely contract their own marriages. Other countries are more observant of the classical practice of making the woman's marriage guardian responsible for contracting the marriage, whether by her request or upon his own initiative. Modern legal codes recognize the role of the marriage guardian and the traditional practice, but set some limitations upon the marriage guardian's power. First, many legal codes, including those of Algeria, Bangladesh, Libya, Malaysia, Somalia, Syria, and Yemen, specify that the marriage guardian is not permitted to prevent a woman from contracting a marriage that she desires if that marriage is beneficial to her. In such a case, the legal code allows the judge to override the guardian's objections and authorize the marriage. The only exception is Algeria, which does not permit a judge to overrule the marriage guardian's opposition when the marriage guardian is the father, the girl in question is his virgin daughter, and the marriage is not in her interests. Jordan restricts the right of marriage without the consent of the marriage guardian to a previously married woman who is of sound mind and over the age of eighteen. Second, and perhaps most important, the overwhelming majority of modern legal codes forbid marriage guardians, even fathers, from compelling women into marriages or giving them in marriages without their consent. Algeria, Iraq, Kuwait, Lebanon, Libya, Malaysia, Morocco, Somalia, Syria, and Yemen have declared invalid any marriage concluded by coercion. Iraq, Malaysia, and Yemen specifically require the woman's consent to the marriage. Iraq punishes by detention or imprisonment anyone who coerces anyone else into marriage or prevents them from marrying. Syrian law declares that any indication of reluctance by either party invalidates the offer of marriage.

Another major area of reform in personal status has been the question of the husband's right to polygamy. As discussed previously, classical law grants the husband the right to have up to four wives simultaneously. However, modern legal codes, in recognition of social change and the *Quranic* interest in social justice, have sought to curb this right. Tunisia enacted the most radical legislation in 1957, when polygamy was outlawed entirely. The law was given practical effect by the assignment of one year's imprisonment and a hefty 240,000 franc fine for both the husband and the wife (provided she was aware that marrying the man constituted polygamy) for violation of the prohibition. The government argued that (1) polygamy, like slavery, was an institution whose past purpose was no longer acceptable to most people; and (2) the ideal of the *Quran* was monogamy. Here, the position of the Egyptian reformer Muhammad Abduh was espoused, namely, that the *Quranic* permission to take up to four wives (4:3) was seriously qualified by verse 4:129: "You are never able to be fair and just between women even if that were your most ardent desire." Thus, while the *Quran* technically permits polygamy, the *Quranic* ideal is actually monogamy, because equal treatment of wives has been deemed impossible. Some twentieth century reformers have also noted of the slavery-polygamy analogy that the *Quranic* ideal is a movement toward less slavery over time until it is abolished altogether. Thus, they argue that the same principle should be applied to polygamy, with the ultimate goal being monogamy, particularly as the initial permission of polygamy in the *Quran* placed a severe limitation on what appears to have been an unlimited earlier practice. To date, of Muslim majority countries other than Tunisia, only secular Turkey and the Ismaili Khojas of East Africa have also outlawed polygamy outright.

Other countries have left the technical permission for a man to have multiple wives intact, but have sought to restrict the practice in the name of social justice. The *Syrian Personal Status Act of 1953* was the first legislation of this type. It made a second marriage contingent upon the husband's proven financial ability to support two wives, placing the power to make the decision about the second marriage in the hands of a judge, rather than the hands of the husband. *Law No. 34 of Personal Status of 1975* created a further restriction by requiring a lawful justification for the additional marriage. Algeria, Bangladesh, Malaysia, Iraq, Somalia, Jordan, Singapore, Libya, Morocco, and Yemen all have similar requirements.

Other types of legislation with respect to polygamy demonstrate a concern for ensuring that the first wife is aware of her husband's activities. Such measures arose largely in response to what many have protested as an inherent injustice in the classical practice of polygamy, whereby the first wife would not necessarily know that her husband had married again or the second wife would not necessarily be aware that her husband was already married. Algeria, Bangladesh, Morocco, and Yemen require notification of both the existing and future wives of the pending marriage. In Malaysia, a man must obtain the permission of both his first wife and the appropriate religious office to contract a second marriage. Additionally, the husband and his first wife are required to meet with a judge, who will ascertain the man's ability to support both families and whether the proposed marriage would represent an undue hardship for the first wife. Somalia authorizes a second marriage only in cases of the wife's sterility, the wife's illness with an incurable chronic or contagious disease, the wife's sentencing to imprisonment for more than two years, the unjustified absence of the wife from the matrimonial home for more than one year, or the existence of social necessity (which must be determined and authorized by the Ministry of Justice and Religious Affairs). Also in response to charges of inherent injustice, Algeria and Morocco grant all women the right to petition for a divorce if they suffer harm from the husband marrying a second wife, regardless of whether they have made a stipulation prohibiting the same in their marriage contracts. Iraq grants the wife this right only in cases where the husband has remarried without the court's permission. Somalia allows the wife to petition for divorce only in cases where the first marriage has produced no children, emphasizing the importance of procreation as one of the main purposes of marriage. Yemen adds an interesting further twist to the financial question by allowing any wife to request a divorce in cases where the husband fails to provide maintenance or accommodation owing to his having multiple wives. In such a case, the judge will require the husband to choose one wife to keep and to divorce the others. If the husband refuses, the judge will dissolve the marriages of whichever wives have applied for divorce.

Concerns for social justice and adaptation to modern conditions have also led to the expansion of the grounds on which a wife may petition the court for divorce. Fairly standard provisions of the wife's right to seek divorce tend to follow classical interpretations of the *Shariah* and include cases where the husband suffers from an incurable disease, infirmity, defect, or impotence that prevents him from consummating the marriage; the husband is or becomes insane; the husband is infertile; the husband is sentenced to prison for an extended period of time; or the husband is absent for more than a year without valid justification. Other circumstances under which the wife is entitled to petition for divorce include the husband's refusal to share her bed for more than four months, failure to consummate the marriage, moral impropriety on the part of the husband (e.g., infidelity or addiction to narcotics or alcohol), or discord between the spouses. Perhaps in recognition of the reality of domestic violence, Algeria, Iraq, Jordan, Kuwait, Malaysia, Morocco, and Syria specifically grant the wife the right to petition for divorce if her husband physically harms her.

One of the most important changes in modern legal codes has been the adoption of the Hanbali practice of allowing the wife to make stipulations in the marriage contract, the violation of which grants her the grounds for requesting a judicial divorce. Algeria, Bangladesh, Iran, Iraq, Jordan, Kuwait, Lebanon, Libya, Morocco, Syria, and Tunisia all specify the right of both spouses to stipulate conditions in the marriage contract that they consider to be beneficial, provided that they do not contradict the law or the purpose of marriage. Examples of possible stipulations include the prohibition of the husband taking a second wife, the right of the wife to work outside of the home, and the right of the wife to complete her education.

The Iranian example is probably the most instructive in terms of the legal thinking surrounding the stipulation of conditions. In Iran, all marriage contracts issued after 1982 include a list of twelve conditions that must be signed individually by both the husband and the wife in order to become valid. These conditions are to be read to the couple at the time of the marriage so that they can either ratify or decline them. The two most important conditions are the wife's right to initiate divorce proceedings under certain conditions and, in case of divorce, the equal division between the husband and wife of the wealth accumulated during the marriage. The presence of standard conditions does not preclude the right of the bride to stipulate other conditions, such as her right to continue her education or work outside of the home.

Use of stipulated conditions is based upon the *Shariah* concept of '*asr wa-haraj* (hardship and harm), which permits the lifting of a rule in cases where adherence to it creates hardship. In postrevolutionary Iran, this has been interpreted to allow expanded grounds for divorce initiated by the wife, as long as the format is in keeping with *Shariah* precepts. These conditions include the wife's right to initiate divorce if: the husband fails to support her or fulfill other compulsory duties for at least six months; the husband maltreats her to the extent that continuation of the marriage is intolerable for her; the husband is afflicted with an incurable disease that could endanger her health; the husband is insane; the husband fails to comply with a court order to abstain from an occupation repugnant to the wife and her social position; the husband is sentenced to a prison sentence of five or more years or his failure to pay a fine results in his imprisonment for five or more years; the husband is addicted to anything that is detrimental to family and marital life; the husband deserts her for more than six months without just cause; the husband is convicted of any offense or receives a sentence that is repugnant to the family and the wife's position; the husband fails to father a child after five years of marriage; the husband disappears and is not located within six months of the wife's application to the court; or the husband enters a second marriage without the consent of his first wife or he fails to treat his co-wives equally.

The requirement that the conditions be listed in every marriage contract was based upon experiences indicating that women are not always aware of their legal right to make such stipulations. This practice could be implemented by other Muslim countries wishing to be certain that women are aware of their rights in marriage.

Modern legislators have also worked to redress some of the injustices inherent in the way in which divorce is actually practiced. One example is legislation that declares invalid divorces declared in certain circumstances, such as anger, confusion, drunkenness, intoxication, insanity, weakness, disorientation, or while under coercion. Reform has also occurred in *khul* divorce, which allows a woman to purchase her freedom from the marriage by agreeing to pay her husband a certain sum, often the dowry. In order for a *khul* divorce to be declared, the husband must agree to it. Because historically there have been serious abuses of *khul*, such as demands for exorbitant payments that the woman could not possibly afford, Algeria passed a law limiting the compensation a man could ask for in case of a divorce to the amount of the dower he paid to his wife upon the marriage. This was considered to be a fair limit since the wife was effectively returning to the husband what he had paid to her in order to commence the marriage, in essence symbolizing the end of the marriage by the return of the gift.

Another reform of the actual practice of divorce has been the outlawing of the triple *talaq* pronounced at a single session in Bangladesh, Jordan, Kuwait, Morocco, Somalia, Syria, and Yemen. This is in keeping with the *Quranic* description of how a repudiation should take place—three statements at three different time intervals with the express purpose of creating sufficient opportunity for reconciliation of the marriage. Popular practice circumvented the *Quranic* ideal through the triple pronouncement of repudiation at a single session, leaving the wife vulnerable to the constant threat of immediate divorce. It was in part to redress this problem that modern legislators have prohibited the triple pronunciation at once. The further requirement that divorces take place through the courts has further served to assure not only a sense of public order, but also protection for women in assuring that they are aware of the divorce and are provided with a period for reconciliation. Kuwait and Morocco specifically require that the wife be aware of the divorce in order for it to be valid.

IMPACT OF THE ISLAMIC REVIVAL

One of the most prominent questions with regard to personal status issues under Islamic law has been the effect of the Islamic revival that began in the 1970s and continues through the present. Several countries, most notably Iran, Pakistan, and the Sudan, have made serious efforts to replace secular legal codes with Islamic law, fusing authenticity with modernity.

Iran in particular has proven to be a curious case study for many Westerners, who became concerned by the apparent "reversion" to the past as what had been hailed as among the most progressive secular laws and legal systems in the Islamic world were replaced by "Islamic" legal codes and systems. Westerners and feminists alike have decried what they perceive to be the oppression of women and a turning back of the clock on women's rights, most strongly symbolized by the return to the veil and the enforced segregation of the sexes. However, closer analysis of specific case studies has shown that segregation is not necessarily as strictly enforced as it might initially appear, and that even the veil evokes numerous images and can be interpreted in multiple ways, raising serious questions about whether too much emphasis has been made upon external, visible signs, rather than examining the internal workings, interpretations, and symbols of any given society. Consequently, it is worth looking at the Iranian case in some detail with respect to the impact of legal changes on women's rights and the legal reasoning accompanying those changes.

Prior to the Islamic Revolution of 1979, personal status matters in Iran were governed by the *1967 Family Protection Law,* regarded as one of the most radical reforms of traditional divorce laws in the Muslim world due to its departure from classical Ithna 'Ashari law. The 1967 law raised the minimum age for marriage to fifteen years for girls and eighteen years for boys, and abolished the husband's right to polygamy, *mu'tah* (temporary) marriage, and divorce outside of the court. Family protection courts were established to deal with marital disputes. *Talaq* was abolished and registration of divorce became the responsibility of the courts via Certificates of Impossibility of Reconciliation. Under the 1967 law, men and women had equal rights to divorce. The wife had the right to petition the court for divorce in cases where her husband failed to provide maintenance, contracted a second marriage, or failed to treat his co-wives equally. In order to give each of these provisions an Islamic appearance, the conditions were stipulated as required elements of marriage contracts. An amendment to the law was passed in 1975, raising the minimum ages for marriage to eighteen for girls and twenty for boys, and modifying the financial terms of maintenance provisions for divorced wives.

The *1967 Family Protection Law* was opposed by various factions of the clergy, most notably Ayatollah Ruhollah Khomeini, because of its departure from classical Ithna 'Ashari law. Khomeini went so far as to declare void divorces issued according to the law. Consequently, seven months after the Revolution, a return to Ithna 'Ashari provisions in family matters was declared via the *Special Civil Court Act,* which removed family law cases, including marriage, divorce, annulment, dower, maintenance, custody, and inheritance, from the civil courts and placed them in Special Civil Courts presided over by religious judges. When the social reality of the reversion to strict Ithna 'Ashari law, such as the lowering of the minimum age for marriage for girls to nine Hijra years, reinstatement of temporary *(mu'tah)* marriage, and reinstatement of the man's right to polygamy and unilateral divorce, became apparent (e.g., physical and health dangers for extremely young brides; poor, pregnant young women divorced by their husbands for no apparent reason and left in destitution), many women were able to successfully question the meaning of "Islamic justice" under such a system. They demanded the introduction of laws that would prevent the use of "Islam" as a justification for causing injustice and misery. The result of this campaign was Khomeini's introduction of a new family law—one of the most advanced marriage laws in the Middle East.

The new Civil Code combined Ithna 'Ashari legal precepts with modern reformist tendencies. Rather than a simple return to classical practice, the new law represented an attempt to adhere to classical legal precepts in light of modern conditions. For example, although Ithna 'Ashari law recognizes only the husband's impotence as just cause for the wife to petition for judicial divorce, current legislation allows the wife to petition for divorce on the basis of either her own specific stipulations entered into the marriage contract or certain stipulations that are printed in every marriage contract as standards required by the government for the couple to discuss and negotiate. This is a clear step toward educating women about their rights while providing the proper legal apparatus to make enforcement of those rights possible. It also resolves the main problem that the *ulama* found with the *1967 Family Protection Act*. Under the 1967 law, clauses limiting polygamy and the husband's unilateral right to divorce were automatically inserted into every marriage contract, regardless of whether the man agreed to them. Because they emphasized marriage as a negotiated contract, the *ulama* considered mandatory clauses not subject to agreement by the parties involved to be un-Islamic and illegal. Consequently, under the new legislation, although the conditions are all listed in the contract, it is necessary for the husband to agree to the conditions individually, entailing a process of negotiation. Further rights for women include the provision that the wife is entitled to up to one-half of the wealth acquired during the marriage in cases where the husband wishes to divorce his wife without any fault on her part. However, it should be noted that this condition is one of the twelve mandatory conditions listed in the marriage contract, meaning that it only becomes effective when both the husband and the wife agree to and sign it. Without their acceptance, the condition does not apply.

Muslim feminists in Iran also have proven to be particularly adept at inserting themselves into religious debates about legal issues to work for greater balance in gender rights. For example, departing from the accepted legal principle that a husband has no right to his wife's labor or property, they have argued that, in the case of divorce, the man should compensate his wife for the labor she has contributed to the management of his household. This argument was passed into law in December 1992, rendering the cost of divorce for men much higher and providing the grounds for women to achieve better financial and legal settlements than was previously the case. It has also served to obtain recognition of and financial compensation for women's contribution to marriage and household management, putting the power of the law behind the contention that Islam does not support the exploitation of women in any way, even for the sake of their husbands and children.

Other major recent achievements in women's rights in Iran include the establishment of the Council of Women's Affairs reporting directly to the president, a women's legal advisory in the Parliament, the appointment of women advisors to aid judges in divorce and custody suits (although women still cannot themselves serve as judges), the appointment of a woman district governor in Sarvestan, the appointment of a woman as one of President Mohammed Khatami's vice presidents, and the lifting of the restriction against women leading congregational prayers in cases where only women are present. Clearly, women have been able not only to participate in civil and religious society, but they are also active participants in the reinterpretation of Islamic law and its meaning in women's lives today. The Iranian example not only disproves facile assumptions of backwardness and oppression for women under a religiously oriented regime, but sheds light on creative approaches to the inclusion of women as active participants in many different arenas.

INHERITANCE

Some of the patterns evident in legislation regarding marriage and divorce are also apparent in legislation addressing inheritance. There has generally been an increasing emphasis upon written documentation, rather than strictly oral witnessing, and the placement of authority in inheritance matters with the courts, rather than with custom and tradition. Iraq, for example, requires that wills be written and either signed or thumb-printed in order to be valid. Notarization is further required if the legacy in question exceeds 500 dinars.

Many countries have reformed classical inheritance law so as to protect and even enhance the rights of women and to provide greater freedom for the testator to bequeath certain portions as he or she wishes. For example, while classical interpretations of Islamic law do not permit bequests to an heir, Sudan and Iraq, like Egypt, allow the testator complete freedom to make whatever legacies he or she wishes within the bequeathable one-third of the estate. Tunisia and Somalia allow a testator to make bequests either in favor of an heir or exceeding one-third of the estate, but only if the other heirs agree to it after the testator's death. Tunisia further provides that, in the event that there are no heirs and no creditors, a bequest, even if it is for the entire estate, is to be carried out, rather than turn the estate over to the state.

Some countries have also adopted the reformist pattern of prioritizing the rights of the nuclear family over those of the extended family, particularly in cases where women are the primary beneficiaries. For example, Iraq allows female descendants to exclude any collateral male agnates in inheritance matters. This represents a major change from classical law, which stipulated that a daughter or son's daughter was entitled to only one-half of the estate (or if there are two daughters, two-thirds), with the remainder falling to a distant agnate. Tunisia also adopted a law allowing a daughter or son's daughter to exclude the collateral male agnate.

Reforms have also been introduced that favor wives over other inheritors. Tunisia rejected the classical Maliki provision that turned over to the public treasury any residue of the estate if there were not enough heirs to take up the full estate. The Tunisian reform allows the wife to share in the amount of the residue. Sudan, Egypt, Syria, India, and Pakistan have also adopted this measure.

Syria, Morocco, and Tunisia, like Egypt and Pakistan, have adopted a system of obligatory bequests to reinforce the right of grandchildren whose parent has predeceased the grandparent to inherit the portion that the parent would have inherited had he or she been alive. However, Syria and Morocco confine the application of the principle to the children of the deceased's son. The children of the deceased's daughter do not benefit. Tunisia limits the obligatory bequests to cases where the grandparent has not already specified a bequest or gift to the grandchild(ren) in the amount of the obligatory bequest. The total amount to be inherited by the grandchild(ren) cannot exceed one-third of the estate.

The most sweeping reforms in inheritance laws with respect to women occurred in Somalia, which set males and females, including husbands and wives, on completely equal footing in matters of inheritance. This was a complete break with the classical practice of women being allowed only one-half of the amount that men inherited. Somali family law also clearly favors the nuclear family over the extended family. In the event that there are no children or grandchildren, Somali law grants one-half of the estate to the widow or widower. This amount is reduced to one-fourth if there are children or grandchildren. If the heirs are the spouse, mother, and father, the spouse receives one-half of the estate, and the mother and father one-fourth each. Somali law also specifies that if the deceased leaves only a parent, the parent is entitled to inherit the entire estate, regardless of gender. Otherwise, if there are children and grandchildren, the amount is reduced to one-sixth for the parent. Likewise, if the deceased leaves only a sibling, whether half or full, he or she shall inherit the whole estate, regardless of gender. If there is more than one sibling, the estate is to be equally divided, again regardless of gender. The same applies in the case of a child; regardless of gender, the child inherits the entire estate or the estate is to be divided equally between the children (or grandchildren if there are no surviving children).

Clearly, although gender equality has not yet been achieved across the board in matters of inheritance, some reforms have been undertaken to extend the rights of daughters, wives, and sisters as heirs. Reforms in inheritance law have noticeably lagged behind reforms in marriage and divorce laws, which have made much greater advances toward expansion of women's rights. Perhaps some of the conceptual concerns that have influenced marriage and divorce laws in the Islamic world—concern for social justice and the protection of women from destitution—need next be applied to matters of inheritance.

Muslim Minorities Living in Non-Muslim Majority Countries: The Case of India

The previous analyses focused on Muslims living in Muslim majority countries, where matters of personal status remain subject to Islamic law, however the country in question interprets it, with the full support of the state. At the beginning of the twenty-first century, Muslims living in countries where they are a minority are also debating and, in some cases, campaigning for the application of Islamic law in matters of personal status. From the United States and Europe to Southeast Asia, Muslims find themselves torn between loyalty to their country and its civil, secular laws and allegiance to their religion and its laws. The case of India is particularly useful in providing an overview of issues and trends current in Muslim minority communities and their ongoing struggle for Muslim identity in non-Muslim societies.

Muslims in India enjoy recognition of some of their personal status laws, although this is often a matter of personal choice, rather than overarching legislation. For example, Muslim marriages are normally subject to Islamic law unless the couple chooses otherwise. Unlike most Muslim majority countries, registration of Muslim marriages and divorces with civil authorities is not currently a requirement in India. Rather, it is considered a private matter between private individuals unless the couple decides to register their marriage under the *Special Marriage Act of 1954*. Marriage under this act renders the marriage a civil, rather than religious, matter, subject to India's secular divorce and inheritance laws. This entails the prohibition of polygamy, since Indian civil law has outlawed polygamy on the basis of its inherent injustice to women. India requires registration of all interreligious marriages under the *Special Marriage Act* so as to eliminate debates about which religious law is to be followed.

While India allows religious pluralism and grants each religion the right to follow its own religious laws, there remain inconsistencies and flaws within the administration of the religious laws that permit abuses. For example, because registration of marriage and divorce is not required for Muslims, the checks that have been placed upon the husband's unilateral right to divorce his wife in other countries, such as the prohibition of the triple *talaq* pronounced at a single session, do not exist in India. Furthermore, the prohibition of polygamy under secular civil law is not applicable to Muslims who are not married under the *Special Marriage Act*. Muslims are the only religious group who have retained the right to polygamy when married under their own religious law, although this right is tempered by legislation allowing the wife to petition for divorce on the grounds of cruelty if her husband takes a second wife and permitting the wife to stipulate a condition in her marriage contract forbidding the husband from taking a second wife.

Another example of inconsistency between Islamic religious and Indian civil law is the civil prohibition of child marriages. The current minimum marriage ages in most of India are eighteen years for females and twenty-one years for males under civil law. Nevertheless, because Muslim marriages are exempt from secular law unless a couple chooses to apply it, child marriages remain valid and the Islamic rules regarding marriage guardians continue to be operational. The only check that exists on child marriages under Islamic law is the option of puberty, which minor wives may assert upon reaching their majority, provided that the marriage has not been consummated. Since Hindus adopted a similar law—the *Marriage Laws (Amendment) Act of 1976*—this might be an area where a consensus between different religious groups could be reached to produce a single, standard, universal law.

The most serious recent debates about Islamic personal status law have focused on the central issue of which law is to be considered primary—religious or civil. Some have argued that religious law, by its inherently divine nature, overrides and supersedes any man-made law. Others have argued that the need for national cohesion and identity necessitates the primacy of secular civil and constitutional law over personal religious beliefs, as citizenship and adherence to a common law are intended to be the common links that bind the nation together.

These debates have come to a head in recent years in cases addressing the husband's financial responsibilities toward his wife in case of divorce and the controversial issue of dowers and dowries in India. As noted previously in the discussion of Pakistan, dowry and lavish weddings have long been recognized as the source of serious social problems on the Indian subcontinent, since family pride and the desire to procure a suitable marriage have often resulted in the bride's family incurring substantial debts in order to provide substantial gifts and a lavish wedding reception. For this reason, India outlawed dowries altogether in the civil *Dowry Prohibition Act of 1961*. However, the Muslim practice of *mahr* was exempted from this civil act owing to (1) its religious nature, as clearly prescribed by the *Quran,* and (2) its status as the absolute property of the wife, which is to be provided to her by her husband, thus distinguishing it from a dowry proper that the bride's family must normally provide to the couple.

There are two major issues surrounding the practice of *mahr* in India today. First, although marriage contracts always specify the *mahr* owed to the woman and *mahr* is recognized as the husband's legal obligation to his wife, in India, this is in reality merely a paper transaction. Most Indian women never collect their *mahr* in practice, whether at the time of the marriage or after the husband's death when any unpaid portion would normally become due to the wife prior to the distribution of the estate. Ironically, it is the very fact that women's rights with respect to *mahr* and inheritance are not observed that has led women activists to challenge the notion of the man's right to polygamy on the basis of the *Shariah*. Many women have noted the selective application of the *Shariah* in favor of men, while ignoring the financial compensation to which women are entitled.

Second, the exemption of *mahr* from the *Dowry Prohibition Act* led to the declaration according to the *Criminal Procedure Code of 1973* that payment of the deferred portion of the *mahr* upon divorce exonerated the Muslim husband from his liability under Islamic law to provide the wife with maintenance during *iddah*. The problem arose from Section 125 of the code, which included divorced wives in the definition of "wife," making Muslim husbands potentially liable for maintenance of their divorced wives beyond the waiting period until the wife either died or remarried. Indian Muslims serving in Parliament responded with the passage of Section 127 (3)(b), which specifically states that Muslim husbands are not liable to pay continued maintenance to the wife if she has received the whole of the sum customarily payable upon divorce. Non-Muslim judges understood this to mean that a woman who had been paid the deferred portion of the *mahr* was consequently not entitled to maintenance during the waiting period in addition to the *mahr*. However, because amounts of *mahr* are typically set at very low sums, in practice, receipt of the deferred portion of the *mahr* has proven insufficient for the wife's maintenance.

The issue of *mahr* as maintenance came to the courts in the *Bai Tahira* case, AIR SC 362 (1979), which was tried on the basis of *mahr* being insufficient for the wife's maintenance. Because the court found no provision in Muslim law addressing a divorced wife who is unable to maintain herself, the court ruled that Indian civil law overrides religious personal law. Therefore, the court turned to the Criminal Procedure Code, which states that the customary sums payable upon divorce must be sufficient to maintain the divorced wife beyond the waiting period. The judges asserted the primacy of social obligation over ritual religious exercise as being in the best interests of society. This ruling then became a general rule applicable to all Muslim husbands, requiring them to maintain their divorced wives until the wife either died or remarried and opening the floodgates for other divorced Muslim women to seek redress from the courts when the amounts of *mahr* they received upon divorce were insufficient for their survival.

The matter came to a head in *Shah Bano v. Mohd. Ahmed Khan*, AIR SC 945 (1985). In this famous case, the former husband of Shah Bano, an elderly Muslim woman who had been married for many years, argued that he should not have to provide her with maintenance beyond the waiting period as required by Indian civil law because his religion did not require it. The former husband spoke for many Muslim men in protesting what he felt was an unfair financial burden that violated the letter of Islamic law. Because Shah Bano was left destitute following her waiting period, the chief justice of the Supreme Court ruled in her favor, commenting that, under Section 125 of the *Criminal Procedure Code*, the husband is responsible for providing his divorced wife with maintenance when she has no means of livelihood. The chief justice stated that this provision was in keeping with the spirit of the *Quran*, which enjoined a man to look after his wife. The judgment also asserted the primacy of the Constitution as applicable to all citizens, over personal religious codes.

The case initiated great controversy for several reasons. First, the judgment assisted only those women who were unable to maintain themselves after divorce, rather than women across the board. Consequently, some women activists felt that the ruling did not go far enough in extending the right of alimony to divorced women. Second, Muslim men objected to what they felt was a violation of their *Quranic* rights by extending the payment of maintenance beyond the waiting period. They argued that Islamic law required them to provide maintenance only during the waiting period and that no Constitution or court should have the right to demand that they pay beyond that. They also objected to the fact that a secular court ventured into interpretation of the *Quran*. However, Muslims who supported the judgment noted that the *Quran* itself states that a divorced wife has the right to reasonable and fair provision after divorce, so that the judgment was not necessarily a contradiction of *Quranic* principles. Third, the chief justice asserted that the Constitution, as a secular law designed to provide security against vagrancy and destitution, should not be made subject to religious dictates, but applied to all religions across the board. Although the argument was not made in court, it is of interest that the issue here really is a question of whether any legal code can require a person to do more than the absolute minimum required by his or her personal religious beliefs. The *Quranic* injunction that the husband should provide maintenance for his divorced wife during her waiting period is a minimum requirement to be expected of all husbands. The *Quran* never states that it is illegal or impermissible for a man to pay maintenance beyond that. Consequently, whether an extension of the responsibility beyond the minimum required by religious law is actually a violation of that law is open to question.

In the end, the ruling in favor of Shah Bano was overturned and the *Muslim Women (Protection of Rights on Divorce) Act of 1986* was enacted. This act was considered by many women activists to be a backward step, because it not only confirmed the restriction of the Muslim husband's responsibility to his divorced wife to "reasonable and fair provision and maintenance" during the waiting period after the divorce and while she holds custody over the children, but it then absolved the husband from further financial responsibility for her by shifting that responsibility instead to her natal family and children. In a case where the natal family or children are unable to provide for the woman, the woman is to be maintained by the State *Wakf* Boards. The last provision was made in response to concerns that divorced Muslim women could potentially become destitute, as there is no state welfare system in India.

Women activists have noted that the men responsible for formulating the law preferred to place responsibility for a divorced woman's maintenance on her own family and charitable institutions rather than on the former husband, essentially protecting their own interests and reaffirming the notion that the woman has no right to expect any financial benefit beyond her *mahr* and maintenance from marriage, regardless of the length of the marriage or the wife's contribution to her husband's or household's achievements. Furthermore, the law makes no distinctions according to the reason for the divorce or who initiated it.

The *Muslim Women Act of 1986* is a prime example of adherence to the letter of classical interpretations of Islamic law, rather than concerns for social justice. In this respect, Islamic law as practiced in India does not reflect the reforms and progress made by Muslim majority countries with respect to women's rights. Finally, the 1986 law represents the primacy of personal religious law over secular civil law, allowing one religious group to override the constitutional precepts that other citizens are expected to follow.

The *Muslim Women Act* was amended by Bill No. 83 in 1988. In response to male concerns about potential abuses of extended maintenance, the amendment specified that maintenance owed by the husband ceases at the end of the woman's waiting period unless she has children under the age of two. Also in response to male concerns about potentially having to pay maintenance to a wife who initiated the divorce, the amendment specified that, in cases where the woman initiates the divorce, the terms the husband and wife agreed to at the time of the divorce are to prevail over any laws. Once again, this allows personal arrangements to override constitutional law. In such cases, the wife has recourse to the law only when she is denied something that was lawfully rewarded to her. Finally, the responsibility of the State Wakf Boards to provide for destitute divorced women was narrowed to provisions available from money received specifically for the purpose of assisting destitute divorced women or money received for general charitable causes, limiting the potential financial resources available to such women. The argument supporting the restriction was that the civil government has no right to interfere with religious charitable organizations, and use of *waqf* funding for destitute divorced women has no precedent in Islamic law. To date, the State Wakf Boards have never issued any payment of maintenance to any woman.

The 1986 law met with vehement protests and charges of unconstitutionality because of its departure from the guidelines of the *Criminal Procedure Code.* Women activists protested allowing any religion to override rights granted to women under state laws, which essentially granted interpreters of religious laws the right to negate civil law at will. Hindus expressed concern that India is encouraging the fracture of national cohesion along sectarian and communal lines by permitting the violation of what is supposed to be a single, universal, secular law based on a constitution applied to all Indian citizens. Muslims, for their part, claimed that the passage of the *Muslim Women Act of 1986* reflects government respect for the equality of all religions and regard for the religious rights of minorities, heralding an important turning point for Muslim status in India. The arguments are representative of the major debates currently surrounding Muslim minorities in non-Muslim majority countries.

Perhaps in response to some of these concerns, particularly the matter of religious versus civil laws, some major changes in the interpretation of divorce laws in India have occurred in recent years. *Shahida Khatoon v. Khalid Ahmad,* Lucknow (1988) is an instance of legal enforcement of male financial obligations to a divorced wife, even though the couple had originally reached an alternative agreement. Shortly after her marriage in 1987, Shahida Khatoon arrived at the matrimonial home and discovered that her husband was already married and that the first wife was living with him. A private agreement to divorce was reached, whereby Shahida Khatoon agreed to forego her claims to *mahr* and maintenance during the waiting period in exchange for the return of her dowry (valued at 68,980 rupees). The husband subsequently refused to turn the dowry over to the wife's brothers and the police chief. Consequently, Shahida Khatoon turned to the courts to enforce the agreement. The court not only ordered the return of the dowry, which Islamic law recognizes as the woman's property, but also ruled that the husband was further required, by his own religious law, to fulfill his financial obligations to his divorced wife, including *mahr* and maintenance during her waiting period. This case is particularly significant for its upholding of Islamic law, despite the private agreement of the parties to other terms.

Since this case, several other cases have been resolved in the favor of the female petitioners. In *Fahmida Ahmed v. Shafaat Ahmed,* Lucknow (1988), filed under the Muslim Women Act of 1986, the court awarded 2.1 million rupees to Fahmida Ahmad for dowry articles, 52,000 rupees for *mahr,* 30,000 rupees for reasonable and fair provision for maintaining her standard of living, and 1,000 rupees monthly as maintenance during the waiting period. In 1989, Rukhiya of Trikarpur was awarded 90,500 rupees by the judge of Payyanur as recompense for the 15,000 rupees and twenty gold sovereigns given by her parents at the time of her marriage. All of these cases demonstrate the court's support for upholding male financial obligations according to Islamic law. They also have put into effect the principle of *mahr* as a debt that can be legally enforced by the court in the event the husband does not pay. However, it should also be noted that only in the case of Fahmida Ahmad did the court include an assignment of alimony enabling her to maintain her standard of living. Neither of the other two cases include a settlement for alimony. Consequently, it would be a mistake to assume that these cases represent anything more than a legal enforcement of male financial responsibilities as outlined in Islamic law. Nevertheless, the significance of the civil court's upholding of religious laws should not be overlooked.

In conclusion, the case of Muslim minorities in non-Muslim majority India presents current issues for Muslim minorities elsewhere, including the central question of the primacy of civil versus religious law with respect to personal status issues and the potential viability of legally recognized religious pluralism. It is also clear that the question of who is to interpret Islam in any given context, particularly with respect to the right of women to participate in the decision-making process, is one that requires serious consideration if Islamic law is to be uniformly practiced within the country.

Legal Methodologies of Reform:
A Critical Analysis

EGYPT

A study of modern Muslim law reform in Egypt reveals three specific legal mechanisms employed to provide an Islamic basis of change: *siyasah shariyyah* *(Shariah* rule), *takhayyur* (selection, preference), and *talfiq* (patching together).

Because Egyptian reform in family law was accomplished through government legislation, the *siyasah shariyyah* power of the ruler or government was used to provide Islamic or religious justification. This doctrine of Islamic public law grants the political authority the prerogative power, whenever he sees fit, to take administrative steps in the public interest in order to ensure a society ruled according to the *Shariah*. Thus, full judicial power rested in the sovereign's hands, allowing him to determine the organs of legal administration, as well as the extent of their jurisdiction. Such discretionary powers were granted to the ruler in order to ensure that the spirit of *Shariah* rule was present in the state in areas that were either not covered or were not covered sufficiently by the letter of the law. For example, child marriages could be discouraged by indirect means, namely, restricting the competency of the court to hear only cases in which the spouses were old enough to have received an official marriage certificate.

A more widespread application of *siyasah shariyyah* involved the government's selection of one legal doctrine from among the variant opinions of the four Sunni law schools and its prescribing that it also be applied by the courts. The practice of *takhayyur* was the basis for this activity. Originally, *takhayyur* referred to the right of a Muslim to select and follow the teaching of a school of law other than his own with regard to a particular transaction. The reformers took the principle and applied it to legislative reform. A prominent example was the Egyptian reform legislation of 1920 and 1929, which established grounds for divorce based on Maliki opinion. The *siyasah shariyyah* power of the political authority was then invoked to pass legislation that required the courts to apply the "preferred," or "selected," Maliki opinions. This principle has subsequently been used by other countries in similar ways to achieve similar reforms. For example, Algerian family law is largely based on Maliki principles, but specifies in *Article 222* of *Law No. 84–114* that the sources of the *Shariah* (i.e., the *Quran*, the *Sunnah* of the Prophet, and opinions of any of the Sunni or other law schools) are to be consulted in order to determine the most appropriate solutions to problems. Libyan law specifies the same principle in *Article 72* of *Law No. 10 of 1984*.

Whereas *takhayyur* traditionally was restricted to selection of the dominant opinion of another law school, the reformers extended it to the adoption of an individual jurist's opinion. For example, regarding Egypt's *Law No. 25 of 1929*, jurists wishing to correct an abuse that resulted from the formalistic positions of the predominant views of the four schools turned to Ibn Taymiyah of the Hanbali school as the main source of the regulation that the effectiveness of conditional expressions of divorce was contingent upon intention and not mere utterance of a divorce formula. This principle was subsequently adopted by other countries to invalidate divorces declared under particular circumstances, such as states of anger, intoxication, etc., since the divorce would have been declared when the husband was not in a clear, rational emotional state and might have said something he did not mean.

An even more innovative method of reform, from the viewpoint of classical law, was *talfiq*, a variation of *takhayyur*. By this eclectic process, the views of various schools or jurists are combined to form a single rule or law. A clear case of *talfiq* may be seen in *Article 17* of Egypt's *Law of Waqf of 1946*. This principle is also evident in the legal codes of other countries, most prominently the most recent of all legal codes, Yemen's *Personal Status Law, Law No. 20 of 1992,* which draws on rules and principles from all four Sunni schools of law.

Egyptian reformers have always scrupulously sought to provide a rationale that, formally at least, appeared to follow *(taqlid)* authoritative teachings of the past. However, the use of *talfiq* in drafting *Article 17* demonstrates the tenuousness of this method. This usage is problematic for two reasons: first, a traditional condition for the practice of *takhayyur* was that the person not combine teachings, but rather follow the predominant opinion of another school; and second, the position of the schools is applied out of context. The doubtfulness of the reformers' claims is evident in the fact that the Hanbali school considered temporary *waqfs* invalid, and so regarded the ownership of beneficiaries to be simply a nominal title. Despite this fact, because they were so anxious to clothe their reform in the mantle of traditional authority, the reformers employed a methodology that claimed formal adherence to past authorities, but actually introduced a substantial material change in the law.

This review of the methodology upon which twentieth century reforms in Egyptian family law have been based shows a deep concern that the legal changes not be viewed as the product of *ijtihad* (reinterpretation). Theoretically, reformers following Muhammad Abduh might advocate Islamic reform through the use of *ijtihad.* In practice, however, Egyptian reforms have been limited to legal mechanisms such as *siyasah shariyyah, takhayyur* and *talfiq* and, as we have seen, these have often been misapplied in an effort to give the appearance of following past legal doctrines. While the motives of reformers might be laudable, the methodology is questionable. One might argue that given the exigencies of the times, such tactics were justified in order to achieve the required reforms. But the long-range value of such methods is negligible, since they do not contribute to a systematic Islamic rationale for legal reform that in the long run could give consistency to substantive legal change. As will be discussed in the next chapter, an Islamic rationale for legal reform can be found in the sources of jurisprudence that were originally responsible for the development of Islamic law.

PAKISTAN

While the aims of Muslim reformers in the Indian subcontinent were similar to those of the Egyptians, there were important differences in their methodology, which has included both legislative and judicial means.

Legislative change in Pakistan, like that in Egypt, might rest on the *siyasah shariyyah* power of the government. However, the reformers' use of *takhayyur* was quite different from Egyptian usage, as can be seen in the *Dissolution of Muslim Marriages Act* of 1939. In this instance, *takhayyur* was employed with far less consistency than was the case in similar Egyptian legislation of 1920 and 1929. Whereas Egyptian laws generally adhered to Maliki doctrine concerning grounds for divorce, the India-Pakistan legislation of 1939 differed from Maliki opinion regarding the scope of desertion, the length of maintenance period, the cumulative nature of maintenance, and the lack of detailed procedures regarding arbitration in maltreatment cases. Furthermore, from a traditional juristic point of view, Pakistan's law of 1939 arbitrarily veered from Maliki opinion and Egyptian legislation by prescribing divorce by judicial decree *(faskh)* rather than judicial repudiation *(talaq)*. This variance is significant not only because of its departure from traditional ways, but also because of change in the effective date of a divorce. A divorce by *faskh* results in an immediate final dissolution of a marriage, whereas *talaq* does not take effect until the expiration of the wife's *iddah* (waiting period). Consequently, in a suit involving maintenance, the Egyptian legislation leaves open the possibility of a reconciliation if during the *iddah* period the husband demonstrates his capability and desire to maintain his wife. Pakistan's law precludes such a reconciliation.

Modern legislative action in Pakistan has demonstrated a new attitude toward change based on social need. The inclusion in the *Muslim Family Laws Ordinance of 1961* of the rule that orphaned grandchildren are entitled to their father's share of a deceased grandfather's estate provides a clear example of reform based upon social need. Whereas the Egyptian jurists in 1946 had achieved this reform indirectly by introducing it in the law of bequests (for which they could provide a *Quranic* justification), the Pakistani legislators directly reformed the law of inheritance despite a lack of any basis in traditional law. This action was rationalized on the grounds of social desirability and a lack of any prohibition in the primary sources of Islamic law (the *Quran* and the *Sunnah* of the Prophet).[67]

A second means of reform peculiar to Anglo-Muhammadan law occurred through the operation of the courts. Technically, the courts of Pakistan were merely to apply the law as detailed in authoritative legal manuals, not to create or expand it.[68] However, several factors influenced a departure from classical law. The judiciary in the subcontinent was not as learned in legal texts as *qadis* of the Middle East, for whom Arabic, the language of legal manuals, was a mother tongue. Most important, from 1772 through most of the nineteenth century, the justices were British. Not until the late nineteenth and twentieth centuries were Muslims appointed to the bench. In any event, all justices were trained in the British legal system. Accordingly, British legal principles, especially those of justice and equity, were employed. Thus, while traditional law was respected, where it was judged insufficient to issue a "just" decision, the courts supplemented the law (departed from strict adherence to Islamic law).

Two primary instances of such judicial legal supplementation concern the inclusion of stipulations in marriage contracts and the rejection of family *waqf*. With the exception of the Hanbali school, the Sunni schools of law do not admit the inclusion of stipulations or conditions concerning the rights of the marital partners. However, the courts in the Indian subcontinent, although committed to follow Hanafi law, have quietly allowed such agreements in Muslim marriage contracts, and this action was not the result of adoption of Hanbali opinion.[69] The second example of judicial interference with traditional law concerned the law of religious endowment *(waqf)*. In 1894, the Privy Council upheld a decision of the High Court that was contrary to Hanafi law of family *waqf*. However, the High Court's clear departure from traditional law in rejecting the validity of family *waqf* was later reversed by *waqf* legislation.

The courts of Pakistan have taken an even bolder position regarding their powers since 1961. As mentioned above, although the principles of justice and equity had influenced court decisions, the function and duty of the court had always been recognized in theory as the application of Hanafi law found in classical legal manuals.

However, a clear departure from this position occurred in 1964 in a decision rendered by the High Court of Lahore in *Khurshid Jan v. Fazal Dad*. The question posed by the court was "Can courts differ from the views of *imams* and other jurisconsults of Muslim law (i.e., the authoritative legal texts) on grounds of public policy, justice, equity, and good conscience?"

After an exhaustive study, the court responded that "if there is no clear rule of decision in *Quranic* and traditional texts . . . a court may resort to private reasoning and, in that, will undoubtedly be guided by the rules of justice, equity, and good conscience . . . views of the earlier jurists and *imams* are entitled to the utmost respect and cannot be lightly disturbed; but the right to differ from them must not be denied to the present-day courts." [70] The court's power to exercise *ijtihad* was again underscored in 1965 in *Zohra Begum v. Latif Ahmed Munawwar*, a case in which the court departed from rules governing custody of a minor. The High Court of Lahore reversed the decision of a lower court and instead allowed a mother to retain custody of her children beyond the ages at which they would usually be turned over to their father. This decision was justified on the basis of the best interests of the child. [71]

The result of these landmark decisions is that the courts of Pakistan no longer view themselves as restricted to following *(taqlid)* the authoritative opinions of the past. Instead, where justice and equity demand, they may exercise *ijtihad* (resort to individual reasoning or interpretation) based on the following criteria: (1) that the decision meets a social need, and (2) that the regulation is not prohibited by the *Quran* and the *Sunnah* of the Prophet.

However, the *ijtihad* of the courts differs from the *ijtihad* of the past, as well as that of many modernists who would base their *ijtihad* not only on social need, but also on *Quranic* values. Such an approach ensures the Islamic basis and character of reforms and distinguishes itself from that of the Pakistani courts whose methodological basis seems indistinguishable from that of rational humanism.

While the reforms introduced through legislation and judicial decision in Pakistan might have been needed, the lack of a systematic Islamic rationale for their introduction creates serious problems. First, it raises questions as to the Islamic character of the laws and the relationship of the reforms to the body of traditional law. Second, following from these unresolved theoretical and methodological questions, the apparent discontinuity of many reforms with traditional *fiqh* leaves them vulnerable to heavy fire from the masses of the population who tend to be more conservative in outlook. For example, strong opposition to the recommendations of the Commission on Marriage and Family Law of 1955 delayed legislation until 1961, and passage of the *Family Laws Ordinance* was followed by continued discontent and debate. Consequently, in July 1963, the West Pakistan Provincial Assembly passed a resolution recommending the repeal of the ordinance. With support from A.P.W.A. and other women's organizations, much of the press, the president of Pakistan, and his law minister, the bill to repeal the ordinance was defeated in the National Assembly (November 26, 1963) after twenty hours of debate.

The continued vulnerability of those aspects of family law reform that lack a rationale rooted in Islamic jurisprudence is evident in Pakistan today. The strong re-emergence of Islam in politics, evident in many Muslim countries in the 1970s, brought together opposition forces in a coalition against the government of Zulfikar Ali Bhutto, culminating in a 1977 *coup d'etat* by General Zia ul-Haq. Zia appealed to Islam to legitimate his rule, declaring legislation implementing the *hudud* punishments for theft, *zina* (sexual relations outside of marriage, including both fornication and adultery), false accusations of unchastity, and consumption of alcoholic beverages and implementing other Islamic measures, such as interest-free banking and compulsory *zakat* and *ushr* taxes. From the perspective of methodology, the most important provisions made by Zia were the establishment of a Federal Shariat Court to examine the compatibility between the *Shariah* and existing laws and legal provisions; the *Enforcement of Shariah Ordinance of 1988*, which declared the *Shariah* as the supreme source of law and the guide for setting policy and law-making in Pakistan; and the appointment of the Islamic Ideology Council, consisting of government-appointed religious and lay experts, to serve as an advisory body to the government on Islamic affairs. The council continues its review and revision of the *Muslim Family Laws Ordinance of 1961*, considering issues that are seen as lacking an Islamic rationale. Three provisions in particular remain under consideration: (1) procedures governing notice of divorce and the mandated period for reconciliation—this notice in particular has been debated in several court cases and, although the regulation has been neither repealed nor abrogated, it has not been enforced since 1988; (2) the requirement that a husband indicate whether his existing wife has consented to a proposed second marriage; and (3) the stipulation that orphaned grandchildren be awarded that share of their grandparent's estate that would have gone to their predeceased parent.

In conclusion, a review of the methodology of the family law reforms in Egypt and Pakistan shows an *ad hoc,* fragmented approach that has employed questionable *talfiq* (patching together), an incomplete following of *takhayyur* (selection), and a claim to *ijtihad* (reinterpretation) not positively rooted in Islamic values but rather negatively based on a lack of conflict with any *Quranic* injunction. The lack of consistency in methodology is reflected in the law itself. For example, while an *ad hoc* measure such as the provision for orphaned grandchildren's inheritance rights met a particular need, it disrupted the law of succession in Pakistan. An orphaned granddaughter of the deceased now excludes the collaterals (brothers and sisters) of the deceased from inheritance. However, the deceased's own daughter would not exclude these same collaterals.

Reformers in both countries face the same basic problems. If reform is to be truly accepted by the majority of Muslims in each country, and if they are to produce a law that is both comprehensive and consistently developed, these reforms must be based on a systematic methodology whose Islamic roots can be demonstrated. As will be discussed in Chapter 4, the dynamic sources for family law reform already exist in traditional Islamic jurisprudence.

4 Toward a Legal Methodology for Reform

THE TWENTIETH CENTURY has been a remarkably significant era in the history of Muslim family law in the areas of both substantive legal reform and jurisprudence proper. Reinterpretation and reform have occurred in both areas. In the name of social progress, reform legislation has been enacted to more equitably meet the changing social and economic needs of women and the family in modern Muslim society. However, salutary as substantive legal change may be, and noble as reformers' motives may have seemed, their solutions have been of an *ad hoc* and piecemeal nature and their legal methodology has been deficient.[1]

The true effectiveness of existing reforms is dependent upon their acceptance not simply by those who legislate but by the entire Muslim community. Thus, reforms must be rooted in a consistent Islamic rationale, one that would demonstrate a link of continuity between change and past tradition. Jurisprudence, the legal principles and methods underlying the reforms, must play a key role because it alone can ensure both inner consistency and historical continuity with the Islamic tradition.

Tradition and Change

Although tradition plays an important role in most cultures, in Islam it has been elevated to an almost sacrosanct status. The reasons for the eventual "sacralization" of tradition are not difficult to identify. The progressive idealization of the history of Islamic law tended to separate the ideal from the real, the immutable from the mutable. The customary practice *(sunnah)* of Arabia, which was incorporated into Islamic law, came to be equated with the *Sunnah*

127

(practice) of the Prophet and thus it was given an unwarranted, elevated religious status. The acceptance of al-Shafii's formulation of the sources of Islamic law also meant a downplaying of the role of reason in the development of law. In classical jurisprudence, the restriction of reasoning *(ijtihad)* to analogy *(qiyas)* created a sense that law was simply the product of specific teachings of the *Quran* and the *Sunnah* of the Prophet plus those doctrines clearly derived from the *Quran* and the *Sunnah* of the Prophet through the application of *qiyas.* Thus, much of substantive law *(fiqh)*, although actually based upon human understanding and interpretation, was imbued with a more sacrosanct character.

Ijma (consensus) also contributed to the process of absolutizing tradition. Although *ijma* served as a check on individual interpretation *(ijtihad)*, the ongoing dynamic, dialectical *ijtihad-ijma* relationship tended to be forgotten. This is reflected in the saying attributed to the Prophet: "My community will never agree on an error." A mechanism created to arrive at authoritative interpretations took on the aura of infallibility. Thus, the *fiqh* found in the manuals of the law schools, much of which was conditioned by historical and social circumstances as well as the use of reason, came to be "enshrined" as a detailed immutable blueprint for society. The doctrine of *taqlid* (imitation or following) was the natural conclusion to this process of the sacralization of tradition.

Ijtihad vs. Taqlid

At the center of the struggle for reform is the doctrine of *taqlid.* According to this teaching, the great putative founders of the Islamic law schools died out and the foundation of new schools *(madhhabs)* concluded at the end of the tenth century. After the eleventh century, all jurists officially followed one of the established law schools, rather than attempting to form new ones, marking the beginning of adherence to *taqlid* (imitation of previous scholars). In this way, then, *ijtihad* as the creative exercise of independent reasoning leading to the foundation of new schools of Islamic law came to an end. Indeed, some scholars and jurists consider the time following the closure of the schools of Islamic law to be an "era of sterility" [2] that continues until today.

However, this does not mean, as is often claimed, that *ijtihad* as the use of independent reasoning to derive new solutions to legal cases has not been practiced at all since the eleventh century. Although the Hanafi school of Islamic law—the predominant school throughout the Middle East—essentially outlawed the use of *ijtihad* in favor of *taqlid* after the thirteenth century and refused to recognize the rulings of those who claimed to exercise *ijtihad*, this was not the practice of the other law schools. Most prominently, the Hanbali school promoted and practiced the continual exercise of *ijtihad* as a required duty of those Muslim jurists who are qualified to carry it out. They argued that the supposed "closing of the gate of *ijtihad*," whether theoretically or in practice, would not only deny to the Muslim community the potential for growth, reform, and social change, but would also leave them remiss in their duties as Muslims.[3] For example, Ibn Taymiyah (d. 1328), the distinguished Hanbali jurist, claimed the right to exercise *ijtihad* and rejected *taqlid*.

This example was followed by some eighteenth century premodernist movements that laid the foundations for modernism in the nineteenth century and the Islamic revival of the twentieth century. Most notably, Muhammad ibn Abd al-Wahhab (d. 1792) and Shah Wali Allah of Delhi (d. 1762) rejected the blind following of medieval jurists and asserted their right to exercise *ijtihad*. Their general plan was to renew the Muslim community by going back to the primary sources, the *Quran* and the *Sunnah* of the Prophet, for direct interpretation. Their efforts provided a principal legacy to Muslim modernism in the late nineteenth and twentieth centuries.

The great Egyptian modernist Muhammad Abduh wrote late in the first decade of the 1900's of the "disease of *taqlid*" that afflicted many Muslims.[4] Abduh often argued that Islam had freed Muslims from blind imitation and enjoined the reasoning of *ijtihad*:

> The *Quran* directs us, enjoining rational procedure and intellectual inquiry. . . . It forbids us to be slavishly credulous and for our stimulus points to the moral of peoples who simply followed their fathers with complacent satisfaction and were finally involved in an utter collapse of their beliefs and their own disappearance as a community. . . . It *(taqlid)* is a deceptive thing, and though it may be pardoned in an animal is scarcely seemly in man.[5]

A similar attitude toward the continued right to *ijtihad* was voiced by the Indian modernist Sayyid Ahmad Khan, and in the twentieth century by the most celebrated Muslim modernist of India-Pakistan, Muhammad Iqbal (1875–1938) when he wrote: "The closing of the door of *Ijtihad* is pure fiction suggested partly by the crystallization of legal thought in Islam, and partly by that intellectual laziness which, especially in the period of spiritual decay, turns great thinkers into idols." [6]

The influence of the doctrine of *taqlid* in legislative reform can be seen in the indirect and often inconsistent legal techniques employed by modern Egyptian jurists to provide a *taqlid* façade and thus avoid the charge of practicing *ijtihad*. In Pakistan, the direct assertion by the Marriage and Family Laws Commission of 1955 of its right to *ijtihad* resulted in a swift and strong reaction from the majority of the *ulama* and other conservative forces that contributed to the delay until 1961 of family law legislation.

Nevertheless, despite opposition from supporters of *taqlid*, it is clear that the call for the rejuvenation of *ijtihad* continues and is justified by proponents as a tool for reviving and restoring Muslim society. Furthermore, particularly with respect to the new developments in science, technology, medicine, and economics that have occurred in the nineteenth and twentieth centuries, an increasing number of Muslim scholars throughout the world have come to recognize the need to apply *Quranic* principles and concepts to new conditions and situations, rather than continuing to adhere to literal or medieval interpretations of verses or situations whose historical contexts have changed over time and space. *Ijtihad* is the means by which these issues can be addressed within an Islamic framework.

The Distinction Between *Shariah* and *Fiqh*

Modern legislators' dependence upon *taqlid* is directly related to an important distinction, often blurred in modern times, between *Shariah* and *fiqh*. *Shariah* is the Divine Law, whereas *fiqh* is the product of human understanding that has sought to interpret and apply the Divine Law in space and time. It is the confusion of this distinction between *Shariah* and *fiqh*, reinforced by the doctrine of *taqlid,* that has led to the overly sacrosanct attitude toward the *fiqh* of the ancestors. Early jurists acknowledged this distinction. An awareness of the profound difference between the perfection of the *Shariah* and the imperfection of man's comprehension of it was well-illustrated by the reluctance of many early jurists to accept the office of *qadi*, a judicial office that would make them responsible before God not only for the interpretation but also for the application of law.

The *Usul al-Fiqh* (Sources of Law) and Islamic Reform

THE *Quran*

The primary textual sources of the law are the *Quran* and *Sunnah* and it is to these that reformers address themselves.

As the very word of God, the *Quran* is the fundamental textual source of the *Shariah*. Not a comprehensive legal manual but rather an ethico-religious revelation, its primary legal value is as the source book of Islamic values: "The *Holy Quran* is the God-made, sublime statement of the ought-to-be . . . the *Holy Quran* contains a complete and perfect world-and-life view." [7] It is the source from which the specific regulations of substantive law *(furu al-fiqh)* are derived through human effort.

The primary area of concern in the relationship between the *Quran* and legal reform is exegesis. A distinctive emphasis that emerges in modernist writings is the necessity of getting at the motive, intent, or purpose behind *Quranic* passages. [8] This approach reasserts the original influence of *Quranic* values in the early development of law and, as such, seeks to renew the process by which *Quranic* values were applied to newly encountered social situations in the first centuries of Islamic legal history. The demands of a rapidly changing society require once more, as in the formative period, substantive legal reforms to meet the needs of the Muslim family. Therefore, a clear grasp of the content of the Divine Will as expressed in the *Quran* and as applicable today is imperative. The fundamental questions facing Muslims today are those that confronted the early jurists: "What is the moral imperative that the *Holy Quran* had brought from God? How does it read when translated into the language of obligation pertinent to the concrete situations of real life?"[9]

The possibility of *Quranic* norms providing a complete basis for legal reform has also been recognized by a Western authority on Islamic law: "The *Quranic* precepts are in the nature of ethical norms—broad enough to support modern legal structures and capable of varying interpretations to meet the particular needs of time and place."[10]

The task of Muslim exegetes is a systematic study of the value system of the *Quran* and the construction of a hierarchy of its ethico-religious values.[11] This method would resolve the problem of *naskh* ("abrogation," the suppression of one *Shariah* rule by a later one where divergent regulations exist), while also supplying a reasonable explanation for the claim of the comprehensiveness of the *Quran*. Most important, it would provide a context within which one could understand the value of specific *Quranic* regulations. Emphasis would be shifted beyond the specific regulation to its intent, to the value it sought to uphold.

Thus, a *Quranic* prescription has two levels of importance—the specific injunction or command, the details of which may be relative to its space and time context, and the ideal or *Quranic* value, the realization of which the specific regulation intends to fulfill. Because the task of the Muslim community is the realization of these *Quranic* values, the goal of jurists is to ensure that *fiqh* regulations embody these *Shariah* values as fully and perfectly as possible. Today, both male and female Muslim scholars are actively engaged in the study of *Quranic* sources and their application to modern conditions and needs, seeking to understand the intent and impact of the verses on the society of its time and how this intent can be applied to the modern context.

This approach could, for example, be applied to a particularly timely problem in family law reform, namely, the equality of the sexes. Verses from the *Quran* have been used by different factions to both support a woman's subservience to a man and to defend her rights of equality. This seeming contradiction can be resolved by an analysis of the relevant *Quranic* verses. One can reduce the concerns of these verses to two basic categories: the ethico-religious and the socioeconomic. On the ethico-religious level, the positions of men and women are on an equal standing, both as to their religious obligations toward God and their peers as well as their consequent reward or punishment: "As to the believers, males and females, they are friends of one another. They enjoin what is good and forbid what is evil, perform the prayers, give the alms and obey God and His Apostle. It is those on whom God will have mercy. God is Mighty, Wise. God has promised the believers, males and females, gardens beneath which rivers flow, abiding therein forever, and fair dwellings in the Gardens of Eden" (9:71–72).[12]

In the socioeconomic sphere, scholars of Islam agree that a major concern of the *Quran* was the betterment of woman's position by establishing her legal capacity, granting her economic rights (dower, inheritance, etc.), and thus raising her social status. However, some also cite *Quranic* verses whose traditional interpretations support what today would be an inequitable position for women. Perhaps the most commonly cited verse is *Quran* 4:34, which some interpret as indicating men's priority over women:[13] "Men are in charge of women, because God has made some of them excel the others, and because they spend some of their wealth."

However, the "priority" attributed to men over women is best understood as originating from their greater responsibility as protectors and maintainers within the socioeconomic context of Arabian society during the Prophet's time. Men, by virtue of their duty to defend and support their extended family members, enjoyed more rights and, consequently, a different status in Muslim society.

The resolution of the dilemma caused by this verse in modern times can be found by applying the principle of the hierarchization of *Quranic* values.[14] The moral and religious equality of the sexes before God represents the highest expression of the value of equality. Furthermore, the ethico-religious equality of women is independent of, and not subject to, change of social situation. This value, then, enjoys a higher degree of priority over any value that is dependent upon a changing social context. The religious obligations incumbent upon man and woman equally belong to the *ibadat* (religious duties due God) regulations, which are not subject to change. In contrast, matters of the socioeconomic sphere belong to *muamalat* (social relations, transactions), which are subject to change.

The assertion of man's "priority," in the sense of "responsibility" for woman, reflects his superiority over her by virtue of her socioeconomic dependence upon him in a particular form of society. The traditional interpretation of man's priority mirrored the influence of customary practice upon some exegetes; that is, traditional interpretations reflect the fact that the exegetes were living in patriarchal societies in which women were for the most part socioeconomically dependent upon men. However, the social situation of women has increasingly and broadly changed in the twentieth century, so that many women are no longer completely dependent upon their husbands for maintenance and protection. Indeed, many women today are pursuing higher education and employment, making them contributors to the household's financial welfare. Consequently, the concept of the "priority" of the husband over the wife in the socioeconomic sphere is subject to change. Some countries, such as Tunisia and Somalia, have recognized this change in contributions to the maintenance of the household and have adjusted their laws to reflect this new reality. In other countries, like Egypt, there is rising pressure for reform to legally recognize the contributions of women to the household by expanding their rights within marriage.

The two prime areas of family law affecting women's equal rights today are divorce and polygamy. Both provide excellent illustrations of the use of *Quranic* values in justifying legal reform.

As was noted in Chapter 2, while the Quran recognized the necessity of divorce, it did so reluctantly, viewing divorce as a last resort where the marriage contract has been strained to its limits. The existence of these values in early Muslim society was further reflected in the traditions of the Prophet Muhammad, such as: "Get married, and do not divorce; indeed, divorce causes the Throne of God to shake!" [15]

The religious and social equality of women with men is a theme well-documented in the *Quran*. Equality is specifically affirmed in the area of divorce: "And women have rights equal to what is incumbent upon them according to what is just" (2:227). While this verse recognizes equal rights of divorce for women, no *Quranic* verse supports the license of divorce presently awarded to males.

Equality of divorce rights is further exemplified in *hadith* literature. The *Sunnah* of the Prophet embodied in these *hadiths* provides a record of the Muslim community's lived experience of *Quranic* values. Where possible, then, while grounding legal changes in *Quranic* values, reformers can also utilize the traditions of the Prophet to ascertain how these values were understood and thus exemplified through the actions of the Prophet. One noteworthy tradition dealing with women's rights to dissolution is that of Aishah, the wife of the Prophet, who reported:

> A girl came and stated that her father had given her in marriage and told her to wait till the Prophet arrived. When the Prophet came, I told him the full story of the girl. He at once sent for the father of the girl and inquired of him whether the facts stated were true, after which he told the girl that she was at liberty to choose or repudiate her husband. The girl replied saying that she chose to retain her marriage, and that she wanted only to know whether women had any rights in the matter.[16]

The very form of this *hadith* reveals its didactic intent—that of affirming women's right of divorce. Another illustration of women's right to a dissolution of an unfavorable marriage is cited in a report from Imam Malik and Abu Daud. "The wife of Thabit bin Qais, Habibah bint Sahil . . . told the Prophet 'I and Thabit cannot pull together.' When Thabit came the Prophet said to him: 'This is what your wife says about you, so leave her.' "[17]

These *hadiths,* if coupled with the previously quoted *Quranic* teaching regarding women's right to divorce, provide an Islamic rationale for legal reform in divorce that will enjoy the twofold support of the traditionally acknowledged material sources of Islamic law, the *Quran* and the *Sunnah* of the Prophet.

To implement this legal reform, citing the inequitable situation that has resulted from the male's abuse of *talaq* and basing oneself on *Quranic* values, a strong case can be made for establishing equal divorce rights by taking away the male's extrajudicial rights of repudiation and equalizing the option to exercise divorce by requiring that all divorce suits be subject to the courts as has been done in a number of Muslim countries.

In addition, based on *Quranic* values, arguments for the restriction and even the prohibition of polygamy are also possible. As was discussed in Chapter 2, the *Quran* had introduced reforms in pre-

Islamic Arabian practice by restricting the prevalent practice and limiting the number of wives permitted a man to four. But even this permission was contingent upon the just treatment of each wife: "Then marry such of the women as appeal to you, two, three or four; but if you fear that you cannot be equitable, then only one" (4:3). Taking into consideration the unrestricted polygamy of pre-Islamic Arabia, as well as the social situation in which this verse was written, namely the battle of Uhud and the deaths of many warriors and consequent problem of numerous widows and children,[18] an argument could be made that the social context of these *Quranic* times made it difficult to go beyond the limitation of four wives. Yet one could conclude with Muhammad Abduh and Ahmad Khan that the ideal of the *Quran,* as seen in the *Quranic* value of impartiality, is monogamy.[19] Thus, the *Quranic* value of "equal justice" for each wife can be used as the criterion for restricting polygamy today. A similar approach has been used in drafting legal regulations that require a married man who wishes to take another wife to demonstrate to the courts his ability to treat his wives equally in terms of finances, as well as love and affection.

Another approach is the observation that the *Quran* tends, for the most part, to promote a gradual approach to resolution of social ills, rather than outright abolition, except in extreme cases, such as the immediate prohibition of female infanticide. According to this line of thought, the *Quranic* limitation of polygamy to four is part of a gradual process intended to lead ultimately to the prohibition of polygamy altogether, similar to what has occurred with the institution of slavery. The suggestion here is that reformers need to move beyond the literal content of the *Quran* and consider instead the greater *Quranic* intent, extending to issues of repudiation, polygamy, inheritance, and the rules for witnessing. In response to the typical justifications for polygamy outside of the *Quran*'s ostensible permission for a man to have up to four wives simultaneously, it has been noted that the *Quran* itself does not mention the case of a wife's barrenness as a justification for an additional marriage. Likewise, the rationale of the need for a legal means for the gratification of male lust has no support in the *Quran,* either. Rather, the *Quran* outlines the principles of self-constraint, modesty and fidelity for both men and women. It has been argued that these responsibilities can best be carried out in a monogamous marriage.[20]

Moving even further, the absolute prohibition of polygamy may be based on the requirement of impartiality and the impossibility of its full realization today. *Quranic* support for this contention is available. In addition to *Quran* 4:3, a corollary verse states: "You will never be able to treat wives equitably, even if you are bent on doing that" (4:129). Therefore, an Islamic defense of the above legal changes in divorce and polygamy could be based upon the argument that a necessary continuation of the ongoing task of Muslim jurisprudence is to ensure that the laws of *fiqh* for each age express *Quranic* values as fully as possible. Subhi Mahmasani, in discussing the reasons for the decline of Muslims, underscores the failure of some early jurists to incorporate *Quranic* values in law as fully as possible: "However some jurists were influenced by dominant pre-Islamic customs . . . and declined to apply in such cases the rulings imposed by the teachings of religion. If they had done so, giving religious and ethical principles more consideration, along with as much implementation in law as had been possible, their attitude would have been closer to the spirit of Islamic jurisprudence and teaching."[21] In effect, then, these reforms may be viewed as taking those *Quranic* values that traditionally had been regarded as moral exhortations for Muslims' personal conscience and incorporating them as legal conditions.

THE *Sunnah* OF THE PROPHET

As has already been indicated in examples of *hadiths* regarding marriage and divorce, an axiological approach can validly be applied to the second material source of law—the *Sunnah* of the Prophet. The *Sunnah* also provided those Islamic values that permeated the development of classical legal theory. To focus once more on these ideals, freeing them where necessary from the limitations of specific details that reflect the space and time context of early Islamic society, would enable the reapplication of these *Sunnah* values in contemporary Muslim society.

The validity of this method is justified by an appreciation of the historical development of *Sunnah* and *hadith*. Twentieth century scholarship has, in fact, demonstrated that the development of Islamic jurisprudence in general and *Sunnah* in particular was a much more dynamic and creative process than classical theory would suggest. Indeed, at the center of the creation of Muslim law by jurists and *qadis* was the application of Islamic values to the concrete social situations facing the community on a wider scale than had even been imagined. Thus, a more accurate historical view provides a corrective for misconceptions regarding the formation and nature of Islamic law. This results, as will be seen, in a rationale or methodology more conducive to Muslim family law reform, as well as Islamic reform in general.

The classical theory of *Sunnah* and *hadith*[22] predominated until the early twentieth century, when Orientalist scholars rejected the authenticity of much of the Prophetic *Sunnah*. Drawing on the investigations of I. Goldziher, D. S. Margoliouth and C. S. Hurgronje,[23] Joseph Schacht in his *Origins of Muhammadan Jurisprudence* concluded that the bulk of the Prophetic *Sunnah* could not be considered authentic in the classical sense because he found no written traces of the *hadith* prior to the eighth century CE.[24] Consequently, Schacht believed that very little information about the Prophet, outside of the *Quran*, was handed down from the past. He maintained that what is called the *Sunnah* of the Prophet is not the words and deeds of Muhammad himself, but apocryphal material originating from customary practice that was back-projected in the eighth century to a more authoritative source: first the Successors, then the Companions, and finally to the Prophet himself.[25]

Schacht's thesis, then, is that the term *Sunnah* of the Prophet actually developed for the first time in the eighth century under the influence of the Traditionalist Movement (those who supported the use of *hadith* as a primary source of Islamic law). He noted that al-Shafi was the first significant jurist who limited the term *Sunnah* (custom or practice) to the verified *Sunnah* of Muhammad, i.e., his model behavior. Schacht maintained that the use of this term gave legal authority to what he believes were later customary practices and traditions. Therefore, according to Schacht, what is called *Sunnah* of the Prophet is not a reliable source of Prophetic norms.

Schacht further held that because al-Shafi had won special status for the *Sunnah* of the Prophet as a material source of law, he had essentially excluded those traditions of the early schools that many believed were true manifestations of the Prophetic *Sunnah*. As a result, many jurists recognized the need to justify and authenticate the traditions they favored. Thus, the fifty-year period following al-Shafii's death witnessed a sudden burgeoning of *hadiths* about Muhammad's actions, which came about in one of two ways, according to Schacht: first, by the original creation of new *hadiths* that were actually contemporary interpretations of what Muhammad would have said or done about some problem; or, second, by the projection of *sunnah*s originating from the Companions or Successors back to the most authoritative source, Muhammad himself.[26] On the basis of his research, Schacht found no written evidence of legal traditions before 722 CE, that is, almost 100 years after the death of Muhammad.

Although Schacht's findings initially were widely heralded as conclusive and helpful in more fully understanding the creative role of the community in the development of Islamic law, his conclusions seem excessive and have been challenged by more recent scholarship. First, to state that no tradition goes back prior to 722 CE creates an unwarranted vacuum in Islamic history. To consider all *hadith* apocryphal until they are proven otherwise is to reverse the burden of proof. Rather, a *hadith* accepted for over ten centuries should stand as reliable until proven otherwise. Furthermore, the discovery of manuscripts and critical analysis of extant materials in the second half of the twentieth century has enabled scholars to partially reconstruct earlier sources, some of which date to the second half of the seventh century CE, or within fifty years of Muhammad's death. "When the evidence is carefully weighed, little doubt remains that a substantial corpus of written *Hadith* existed by at least as early as the first half of the first century AH, while the stage of classified works was in all likelihood reached by the first half of the second century."[27]

Second, the "first century vacuum" theory does violence to the deeply ingrained sense of oral tradition in Arab culture which all scholars, both Muslim and Orientalist, have acknowledged. As Fazlur Rahman notes: "The Arabs, who memorized and handed down poetry of their poets, sayings of their soothsayers and statements of their judges and tribal leaders, cannot be expected to fail to notice and narrate deeds and sayings of one whom they acknowledge as the Prophet of God." [28] As Tarif Khalidi has observed, at the time in question, many believed oral transmission was more reliable than written documentation because it provided a personal link between the current and original transmitters.[29] He cites early *faqihs*, such as Muhammad bin Muslim al-Zuhri (d. 742), who commented upon their own personal dislike of writing down knowledge until they were forced to do so by their rulers in order to make the information available to all Muslims.[30] The transition from oral to written transmission was thus a gradual process, undertaken most notably under the Umayyad caliphate beginning with the reign of Abd al-Malik (r. 685–705) due to the need for more manageable and easily disseminated materials. Written collections of *hadith* were both an efficient means of collection and an effective format for diffusion. This, Khalidi posits, explains why written *hadith* collections became an important literary form during this time period and not previously. It does not mean that the *hadith* did not exist prior to that time.

Finally, what of the science of *hadith* verification, with its specific and detailed criteria for establishing authenticity and authority, that accompanied the compilation of the great *hadith* collections? While it was not foolproof and forgeries certainly existed, the wholesale inaccuracy that Schacht and others who follow him in this accusation attribute to this Muslim science is unjustified.

The central challenge raised for Islamic jurisprudence involves the normativeness of the *Sunnah*. Many scholars have acknowledged that the Prophetic *Sunnah*, while probably in large part authentic in the sense of dating from the first fifty years following Muhammad's death, also reflects the attitudes of early generations of Muslims (actual customary practices). During the two centuries in which the traditions were being compiled and becoming normative, they were idealized as "*Sunnah* of the Prophet." Rather than constituting a stumbling block, this realization presents a dynamic picture of the development of Islamic law that demonstrates the viability of the sources of Muslim jurisprudence as a methodology for change.

Much of the misunderstanding about *Sunnah* results from its long and various usage in history. The original meaning of the base root of the word, *sanna*, is "to open or pave a road, to introduce, or set an example." The secondary meaning is "to follow." *Sunnah* in the sense of first introducing a precedent and second following that precedent was used even in pre-Islamic times.

Although some pre-Islamic customs were rejected with the advent of Islam, most continued—some reformed, some supplemented, and others approved either expressly or tacitly. They could never again be merely the customs of pre-Islamic days because tribal practices and beliefs (i.e., customs) had been accepted or modified by the *Quran* and by the example of the Prophet. Muhammad's judgments, attitudes, and conduct revealed *Quranic* values in concrete form as he lived daily in the community. This concrete revelation set new precedents to be followed—the Prophetic *Sunnah*. These precedents were acted upon as future generations set their own examples or *sunnahs*. It is in this sense that Abu Yusuf, in his *Kitab al-Kharaj*, asks the Caliph Harun al-Rashid "to introduce some good *sunnahs*."[31] The values of the Prophetic *Sunnah* permeated early Muslim society both in themselves (i.e., Muslim works and deeds) and as ideals in light of which new practices were judged and either accepted or rejected.

But just how the reality of the *Sunnah* of the Prophet had been operating through the early generations must yet be described. As has been indicated, the term *"sunnah"* has been used throughout history to describe a number of phenomena. We have discussed the meanings or usages of the term *sunnah* as precedents established by the ancestors in pre-Islamic Arabia as well as the Prophetic *Sunnah* or Muhammad's ideal conduct that superseded and modified the pre-Islamic customs. This led to the *sunnah*, or exemplary behavior, of the earliest generations (the Companions) in the Islamic community, the behavior that grew out of the precedents set by the Prophet. To this list we must add the *sunnah* of the next generation, the Successors, which consisted of their interpretations of law based on the living tradition of the earlier generations and the *hadith*. The interpretations of early jurists in this period who reasoned on the basis of *Sunnah* varied. Disagreement about which incidents in the Prophet's life were more relevant to a certain problem and their application naturally led to differing regional interpretations, and so regional *sunnah* developed. All, however, were ultimately based on Prophetic *Sunnah*.

A significant point to remember is that in early Islamic thought *Sunnah* of the Prophet was far from being differentiated from the *sunnahs* that followed: *sunnahs* of the Companions or of the Successors. People who believed that they were following the Islamic norm would naturally equate the Prophet's *Sunnah* with their own. For example, the early Medinese community viewed itself as the community of the Prophet, having lived directly under the Prophet and his Companions. Quite naturally, they would equate their way of life with the *Sunnah* of the Prophet and would never have occasion to draw distinctions.

Prophetic *Sunnah* served as the point of reference for the Companions, and through their example, for the Successors who followed. The admissibility of an action was judged in the light of the Prophetic ideal, *Sunnah* values. This understanding of Prophetic *Sunnah,* while it adds a more dynamic and creative dimension to the theory developed by medieval Muslim scholars, comes to the same conclusion in its emphasis on the importance of *Sunnah* as a material source of law. The normativeness of *Sunnah* as a source of Islamic values remains, while a more historical and developmental understanding emerges. As for the controversy over whether the *hadith* are actually bonafide narrative reports, the *hadith* themselves suggest the possibility for the formulation of new traditions. Consider, for example, the tradition in which Muhammad says: "Sayings attributed to me which agree with the *Quran* go back to me whether I actually said them or not," or the *hadith* in which the Prophet says, "Whatever of good saying there be, I can be taken to have said it." [32]

These *hadiths* and many others indicate concern not for strict historicity, but rather for sound interpretation of *Quranic* norms. In keeping with this line of thought, Fazlur Rahman describes the *hadith* as "the *Sunnah-Ijtihad* of the first generations of Muslims," [33] a "gigantic and monumental commentary of the Prophet by the early community" which "constitutes an epitome of the wisdom of Classical Muslims." [34]

Thus, despite the question of the historicity of some *hadiths,* they still represent the Prophet-directed vehicle for the interpretation and elaboration of *Quranic* norms. As such, they provide a rich source of Islamic values as lived and realized by the early community. As H. A. R. Gibb has observed: "Study of the *hadith* is not confined to determining how far it represents the authentic teaching and practice of Muhammad and the primitive Madinan community. It serves also as a mirror in which the growth and development of Islam as a way of life and of the larger Islamic community are most truly reflected." [35]

In conclusion, while the result of twentieth century critical studies has been a fuller and more nuanced interpretation of the historical development of *Sunnah* that differs from the classical theory, this does not negate the importance of the Prophetic *Sunnah* in Islamic law and jurisprudence. Rather, a reinterpretation of the formation and nature of Islamic jurisprudence emerges. The result is a dynamic picture of the ongoing process of Islamization which is reflected in the *hadith* collections of the *Sunnah* of the Prophet. This same traditional methodology (as newly understood or rediscovered) contributes to a viable method for contemporary legal reform. The process that was formulated to meet the needs of the classical period suggests ways in which the door of *ijtihad* can be more fully opened and redynamized in the twenty-first century so that *taqlid* can be laid to rest.

Ijtihad

Ray and Qiyas

In addition to the two material sources of Islamic law, the *Quran* and *Sunnah*, the classical sources *(usul al-fiqh)* included *qiyas* (analogy) and *ijma* (consensus). As with the textual sources, the fuller historical perspective of *qiyas* and *ijma* available today enhances their viability as mechanisms for contemporary legal reform by showing their original dynamic nature.

Study of the development and usage of *qiyas* must be placed within the general context of the development of *ijtihad*, of which it is a part. *Ijtihad* means "self-exertion," to exert oneself in understanding and interpreting the *Shariah*. During the period of the early development of Islamic Law, the *ijtihad* was *ijtihad al-ray*, the exercise of "opinion or personal judgment" by the early *qadis*.[36] The history of Islamic law shows that *ray* played an important role in the decisions of the early *qadis* and the functioning of the ancient schools of law. The task of the early *qadis* was the application of local law. Basing themselves on the customs of their locale, as well as *Quranic* norms and available *Sunnah*, the *qadis* would render their opinions via legal decisions. The legal decisions of the courts were almost totally dependent upon the personal discretion of each *qadi* both as to his understanding of local law and the extent of his application of *Quranic* norms.

Ray also played an important role in the early development of the ancient schools of law during the eighth century; it was especially associated with the schools of Iraq.

The jurists of the early law schools employed *ray* in the formulation of new rules. Finding themselves a century after the Prophet in a socioeconomic situation quite different from that of seventh century Arabia, the task of the Iraqis often involved the formulation of Islamic solutions for new problems. Reason was employed to extend divine prescriptions to novel situations. The use of personal judgment became progressively more systematic and disciplined by the use of *qiyas*.

Throughout the dynamic processes described above, the major activity that emerged was the use of reason to apply *Shariah* values derived from the *Quran* and *Sunnah*. These were a determining factor in *qadi* decisions, and most important, constituted the ultimate standard for the process of Islamization undertaken by the ancient schools of law. Furthermore, *Shariah* values continued to occupy a central role in the drafting of Islamic solutions for newly encountered problems: first, in the use of *ray* and, second, even more consistently and systematically with the development of *ijtihad al-qiyas* (reasoning by analogy). The role of *Shariah* values in the process of *qiyas* has aptly been described as: "The deduction, from a *shariah* principle, of the *hukm*, or *shariah* value, applicable to a new problem." [37]

Istislah

The use of reason, in fact, stretched beyond *ijtihad al-qiyas*, which came to be the only form recognized by classical theory. For Islamic jurisprudence was concerned with ensuring the *Quranic* concern for human welfare,[38] justice, and equity.[39] This concern to guarantee that a means be available to restore the spirit of the law should the letter of the law as arrived at through *qiyas* result in a harsh or rigid conclusion resulted in the principles of *istishab* (presumption of continuity), *istihsan* (juristic preference), and *istislah* (public interest).[40] It is this last principle, *istislah*, which seems best suited for contemporary legal reforms, for it provides a greater scope for the exercise of *ijtihad* and clearly puts into perspective the ends of law, namely, justice and equity, and human welfare or public interest *(maslahah)*.

The employment of the principle of *maslahah* as a source of contemporary legal reform was championed by Muhammad Abduh and his follower, Muhammad Rashid Rida,[41] and the Salafiyyah movement, a reform movement initiated by Jamal al-Din al-Afghani (1839–97) and carried on by Abduh and Rida.

The traditional juristic position was that the *muamalat* (social transactions) regulations of the *Quran* and *Sunnah* had rational connotations and that God's purpose in revealing them was the promotion of human welfare. Thus, a jurist should select an interpretation that best accorded with the public interest *(maslahah)*.

Abduh and Rida extended this concept so that in the event that a particular social need was not covered by specific *Shariah* texts, a jurist using his reason might interpret the law in light of the public interest. The result was a method *(istislah)* by which Islamic law might continuously and comprehensively be adapted to changing societal needs.

Istislah can function today in two instances: first, when conclusions arrived at through reasoning by analogy *(qiyas)* seem contrary to public interest; second, where a social need exists and the interest involved has not been covered by any specific *Shariah* texts. This latter usage is relevant in modern Muslim law reform. The introduction of legislation becomes possible provided such legislation is in the public interest and in harmony with the spirit of the *Shariah*, that is, *Shariah* values. The result is a comprehensive methodology for reform which provides recognition of the social welfare dimension of the law as well as its Islamic character. While this approach differs somewhat from the classical formulation (law as the product of the *Quran* and *Sunnah* texts, analogical deductions, and consensus), it is, in fact, more in accord with the actual history of Islamic law in which historical and social influences and needs played important roles.

This use of *istislah* places greater emphasis on the probability of law rather than its infallibility. The greater recognition of the use of reason, in determining a more equitable solution in light of public interest and its concordance with *Shariah* values, underscores the human character and limitations of the substantive law of *fiqh*.

The employment of *istislah* as outlined above would help to resolve a juristic difficulty caused by the position advocated by the majority report of Pakistan's Marriage and Family Laws Commission in 1956.[42] The majority advocated a right to *ijtihad* provided the desired social change was not prohibited by the *Quran*. Such a methodology appeared to lack a positive Islamic rationale and thus seemed simply utilitarian and un-Islamic. However, the same result could be achieved by the advocacy of the principle of *istislah*. Its use would encourage the more positive emphasis on looking to the revealed texts for *Shariah* values to support the legislation, rather than the negative criterion of lack of *Quranic* injunction. A continuity between reform legislation and the Islamic tradition would be more clearly established. In addition, acceptance of the criterion of *maslahah* means recognition that the law can adapt itself should the interests of the community necessitate change. This would assure the Islamic character of a dynamic and comprehensive law.

The Egyptian reform that sought to protect the rights of orphaned grandchildren of the deceased[43] provides a good illustration of the use of *istislah*. In drafting their reform legislation, Egyptian reformers avoided a direct change in the law of inheritance because they could find no traditional authority ostensibly to follow. Instead, they took an indirect route and provided for orphaned grandchildren by introducing the concept of "obligatory bequest" in the law of testamentary disposition. However, a more direct reform in the law of inheritance itself could have been achieved by a twofold argument that satisfied the two criteria for the exercise of *istislah*, that is, public welfare and consonance with the spirit of the *Quran*. First, the general welfare of Muslim society requires the rectification of this deficiency in the law of inheritance so that the rights of orphaned grandchildren are protected. Second, such a change is in harmony with the spirit of the *Quran*, in which the welfare of orphans is a prominent theme.[44] In addition, the general intent of the *Quran* regarding inheritance is to protect inheritance rights, as witnessed by the "inheritance verses,"[45] and not to deprive individuals of their share.

This same basis (i.e., the general welfare of Muslim society and the *Quranic* intent to protect inheritance rights) applies to the Egyptian reform regarding collaterals of the deceased. Through this reform, collaterals were protected by giving them a right of succession equivalent to that of the grandfather of the deceased. As has been discussed, this was done to prevent their exclusion from inheritance in their brother's or sister's estate by their uncle.[46]

Ijma

Because of its purportedly primary role in the supposed closing of the door of *ijtihad, ijma* has often been associated with the stagnation of *taqlid.* Such an understanding can be deceptive if *ijma* is understood as an unchanging Islamic institution from earliest times. In fact, the concept of *ijma* enjoyed a complex history of formulation, best characterized as a living creative process.

The earliest stage of *ijma* was that of the period immediately after the Prophet, when almost every Muslim had been a "Companion" of the Prophet. During this time, *ijma* functioned not as a conscious concept but rather as the agreed-upon practice of the Muslim community living in accordance with the *Quran* and the *Sunnah* of the Prophet. This same situation held true for the next two generations, that of the "Successors," that is, the Companions' children *(tabiin)* and the Companions' children's children *(tabii al-tabiin).*

With the passage of time, the community grew and spread geographically. Muslims increasingly found themselves in differing social situations faced with many new problems. It was during this period that the early law schools developed and that *ijma* as a formal legal principle emerged.

Political and juristic leaders of the early communities in Medina, Iraq, Syria, etc., exercised *ijtihad* (interpretation) to determine new modes of action. The agreed-upon practice of these leaders constituted the *ijma al-aimmah* (consensus of the leaders).

Early *ijma,* then, provided the Muslim community with a living instrument for revision and growth in the creation of fresh law to fit changing times. In the ancient schools of law, the relationship between *ijtihad* and *ijma* was an ongoing process, moving from individual opinion to community approval to accepted practice to difference of opinion, if conditions changed, and therefore to a fresh reinterpretation of *ijtihad* and *ijma*.

Moreover, this process of thinking and re-thinking was itself subject to differing views regarding its nature. Early in its development, *ijma* was more a regional interpretation by the jurists of a particular province. The Maliki school, for example, placed great emphasis on the *ijma* of Medina. Since it was the home of the Prophet, they felt that their *ijma* was a continuation of the Prophet's *Sunnah*. The Hanbalis stressed the *ijma* of the Companions. The Shafii and Hanafi schools believed that *ijma* should be applied not only to the earliest generations but to all times and to all geographical areas.

Ijma contributed to the great diversity of interpretation and doctrine in the Muslim community, a diversity which, as we have seen, clashed with the strong Traditionist Movement *(Ahl al-Hadith)* in the eighth century, with its successful drive for uniformity both in the sources of law and, therefore, in substantive law itself. The *ijma* practiced by the early schools was strongly condemned by al-Shafii for its diversity. He recognized only the consensus of the entire Muslim community as valid and thus insistently told the differing schools, "You do not have agreement *(ijma)* but disagreement *(iftiraq)*." Al-Shafii's conception of *ijma* was radically different from that of the early schools. For them, *ijma* was not al-Shafii's theoretical, and, practically speaking, unworkable, source of law that required a total agreement of all Muslims. The *ijma* of the early schools, linked as it was with *ijtihad* in a dynamic dialectical process, provided a powerful means for the adaptation of law to changing circumstances. But with the increasing power of the *Ahl al-Hadith* and the consequent rejection of original interpretations of the law through *ijtihad,* the organic interrelationship between *ijtihad* and *ijma* was severed. *Ijma* was isolated—no longer in dynamic tension with fresh *ijtihad,* it became a principle of rigid approval which, once made, was considered forever binding.

In the final classical theory of Islamic law, established between the tenth and twelfth centuries, the agreed-upon doctrines of the Hanafi, Maliki and some Shafii schools came to be considered fixed and unchangeable. Henceforth, jurists of these schools were admonished to practice *taqlid,* to follow the established principles of their individual schools based upon the authority of the consensus of the scholars of the time. No new schools of Islamic law were founded after this time, resulting in the general loss of dynamism in the development of Islamic law in the majority of the Islamic world. The Hanbalis and a small number of Shafiis alone maintained an ongoing exercise of *ijtihad* beyond the medieval period.

Among Hanafi jurists, al-Ghazzali (d. 1111) was among the noteworthy exceptions in this process of legal stagnation. He recognized the consensus of the religious scholars *(ijma al-ulama)* of a generation as a source of law and thus continued to acknowledge the possibility of a living consensus. However, the process of general legal stagnation was not reversed.

Modernist Muslim thought has sought to restore *ijma* to its rightful place and thereby re-establish the dynamic dialectic of the *ijtihad-ijma* relationship. Muhammad Abduh, the "Father of Muslim Modernism," was a strong advocate of the role of reason, the right of *ijtihad,* and viewed *ijma* as a consensus of reason that can reasonably be presumed free from error.[47] However, Abduh's concept of *ijma* is less dogmatic than the traditional notion. His idea of freedom from error is more the presumption of a reasonable possibility, based upon the agreement of a generation's most learned interpreters *(mujtahidun),* than the affirmation of an absolute infallibility.[48] Abduh recognized the right of future generations, in view of changed circumstances, to reinterpret the law. In this way, the dynamic relationship between *ijtihad* and *ijma* is restored.

Muslim modernists follow Abduh's position vis-à-vis *ijma* and the question of its infallibility. In essence, no denial of the value and binding power of *ijma* occurs relative to the period in which it occurred. For indeed, the function of *ijma* is to serve as a brake and safeguard on individual subjective *ijtihad,* which by itself is no more than fallible conjecture *(zann),* and either to reject it as erroneous or to approve it as applicable for Muslim society. What modernists reject is an unlimited or absolute infallibility that denies that *ijma* is open to question and change in future generations as societal circumstances change.[49]

Among reformers in the Indian subcontinent, a progressive reinterpretation of *ijma* has occurred in an attempt to adapt it to the needs of contemporary Muslim society. Ameer Ali (1849–1928) advocated the broadening of the notion of *ijma* and its incorporation within the constitutional government of a modern state.[50] This general notion has become progressively more developed in the writings of Muslim reformers such as Muhammad Iqbal (1875–1938), considered by many to be the outstanding twentieth century modernist of India-Pakistan, and Fazlur Rahman.

Iqbal described *ijma* as "perhaps the most important legal notion in Islam."[51] He recommended the transferral of *ijtihad* "from individual representatives of schools to a Muslim legislative assembly."[52] The *ijma* of the community would be equated with the consensus of the legislatures of modern Muslim states.

Fazlur Rahman, former director of Pakistan's Islamic Research Institute and a member of the Islamic Ideology Council, has pursued a similar line of argument. For Rahman, the *Quran* is not a law book, but rather a guide. Within the framework of its general moral principles, the Islamic community is free to develop its legal system. Even those "quasi-laws as do occur in the *Quran* are not meant to be literally applied in all times and climes; the principles on which these legal or quasi-legal pronouncements rest have to be given fresh embodiments in legislative terms."[53] As with most Muslim modernists, Rahman's methodology rests on the dual principles of *ijtihad* and *ijma*, which provide both the dynamism and permanence required to meet the needs of a changing society. *Ijtihad* is that means by which individuals "think out new solutions to problems on the basis of Islamic principles."[54] The Islamic community will then have a spectrum of interpretations to weigh, discuss, and debate. The consensus that emerges from this process is its *ijma*, which will inform new laws passed by the legislature. Should public opinion change, the law is repealed and replaced by one which embodies the new consensus of the community.

What emerges from the equation of *ijma* with the consensus of a modern legislative assembly is a reinterpretation that is significantly different from traditional practice. In the past, the consensus of the community as a whole *(ummah)* or of the major figures in the law schools *(imams)* or of the religious scholars *(ulama)* occurred over a protracted period of time as certain interpretations became more accepted than others and eventually became the agreed-upon practice. This traditional view of consensus is quite different from that obtained through the process of legislation in a national assembly.

Effective change need not require the reorientation of *ijma* advocated by Iqbal and Rahman. Their suggestions regarding the transfer of *ijtihad* to a legislature can be used productively for dynamic legal changes to meet societal needs. At the same time, the difficulties that their method raises can be circumvented by equating the resulting social legislation with *ijtihad* alone and not *ijma*.

It is at this point that the dynamic relationship of *ijtihad* and *ijma* can be restored. *Ijma* provides the test of time and community experience that a new interpretation *(ijtihad)* must undergo in order to ensure acceptance of its long-range value by the community. If the new legislation *(ijtihad)* does not survive the questioning and debate within the community, it will be repealed and replaced. In contrast, should it remain unchanged, then its community acceptance *(ijma)* and authority will be established. However, it is important to note that even this fresh *ijma* may in future generations be subject to renewed *ijtihad* as the dialectical process continues.

An illustration will serve to clarify this process and its importance. The question of polygamy has been a major issue in twentieth century Muslim family law reform. Reformers in most Muslim countries have attempted to restrict the exercise of polygamy through legislation based on their interpretation of *Quranic* values that concludes that monogamy is the *Quranic* ideal and thus should be the community's legal norm. The reform called for would constitute a significant departure from traditional Muslim social and legal practice. Furthermore, it would introduce serious change affecting husbands, wives, and children. Therefore, the acceptance of monogamy as a long-range religious norm must be approached cautiously. To equate a legislative change enacted at a particular point in history by a single act of a legislative group with the *ijma* of the community is a drastic step. The passage of such legislation may be due to fortuitous circumstances in which a strong minority legislates a position repugnant to the majority. Such reform legislation may be repealed soon afterwards, or simply ignored by the majority of the population. Equating such an activity with *ijma* would render the concept meaningless.

Historically, it is possible to view the question of polygamy vis-à-vis monogamy in the contemporary Muslim world as a juncture in the *ijtihad-ijma* dialectic. Throughout the twentieth century, reformers have called for change. Initial draft legislation such as that submitted to and approved by the Egyptian Cabinet in 1927 was vetoed by King Fuad. However, in 1953, *Article 17* of the *Syrian Law of Personal Status* enacted the first law restricting polygamy. Since then other countries, such as Pakistan, have passed similar legislation. The most sweeping legislation occurred in 1957 when *Article 18* of the *Tunisian Law of Personal Status* decreed that polygamy was prohibited.

The debate regarding polygamy in the Muslim world today continues. Personal as well as collective (legislative) *ijtihad* has offered two basic reform positions—restriction of polygamy or prohibition of polygamy. These are juxtaposed against the traditional *ijma* supporting the right of polygamy. Out of this protracted debate, a new *ijma* will emerge.

The use of *ijtihad* and *ijma* to provide a rationale for drafting Islamic law raises two controversial issues: (1) Who possesses the power to make laws? and (2) What is the role of the *ulama* (religious scholars)? Many conservative Muslims would agree that only Allah (God) can make laws and, thus, no individual or elected body can legislate. Most of the *ulama* and their followers would claim that only the *ulama* possess the traditionally accepted qualifications and expertise required to be a *mujtahid* (one who exercises the right of *ijtihad*).

The dispute regarding the power to make laws is again rooted in a failure to distinguish between the immutable *Shariah* (the divinely revealed principles and values) and *fiqh* (that body of law worked out by jurists and therefore the product of human understanding, interpretation, and application), which is historically conditioned and subject to change. Due to the predominance of the doctrine of *taqlid*, the law enshrined in the legal manuals has been viewed, in practice if not in theory, as divinely mandated. Thus, even where conservative religious leaders speak of the possibility of changing certain *fiqh* regulations, in practice they are often loath to do so.

The second issue—who is qualified to interpret Islamic law—is rooted in the *ulama's* assertion of their traditional role as guardians of the law. They claim that they alone possess the traditionally accepted qualifications of a *mujtahid*. Muslim reformers respond that the term *alim* (pl. *ulama*) simply means a learned person. Since there is no ordained clergy in Islam, all Muslims may qualify for this designation. As to the areas of knowledge that a *mujtahid* must possess, reformers maintain that knowledge of the traditional religious disciplines *(Quran, hadith, Shariah)*, is not, and should not be, restricted to the *ulama*. More important, the demands of modernity are such that expertise in many modern disciplines, such as medicine, economics, psychology, and sociology, are also required today, an expertise that falls beyond the competence of most *ulama*. Countries seeking to Islamize their societies, such as Pakistan and Malaysia, have established councils and bodies consisting of both *ulama* and scholars of various lay disciplines, particularly the sciences and economics, to work together to develop laws and methodologies that are faithful to Islamic values, yet reflect the reality and needs of a modern, global society. The leaders of many modern Islamic movements are not traditional *ulama*, but engineers, doctors, lawyers, and professors who seek a rejuvenation of Islam in public life not as a return to a pre-modern past but as a means of revitalizing Islam in the modern world. Many of these leaders and reformers view the traditional *ulama* as obstacles to change—men whose limited training and world view, as well as a tendency to protect their own vested interests, prevent them from fully appreciating the demands of modernity and providing the leadership necessary for Islamic reform. The Iranian reformer Ali Shariati notes that the traditional religious leaders "suppressed true knowledge of religion, and hindered the true understanding of Shii beliefs."[55] Thus, it is likely that reinterpretation of Islam will continue to develop along modern lines and to address modern issues as an increasing number of professionals, both men and women, insert themselves into the debate over the role of Islam in modern society and its meaning for individual believers.

CUSTOM[56]

In seeking an Islamic rationale for contemporary legal reforms, besides the official sources of Islamic jurisprudence, there are "extraneous sources" (from the classical viewpoint) which contributed significantly to substantive law. By far the most important of these is customary practice. A study of the role of custom provides a fuller picture of the sources of the material content of law and helps to explain the existence of certain attitudes and mores evident in classical family law.

Although not officially or theoretically recognized, customary law played a key role in the development of Islamic law. Custom (adah, urf) in pre-Islamic Arabia, as in many early traditional societies, served as law. For the majority of the Arabs, custom, the body of unwritten rules that developed and was passed down through the generations, provided the positive laws of their society. Normative legal custom constituted the sunnah (path or way) of the tribe.

The advent of Islam signaled a profound and radical change in Arabian society. Yet, while recognizing the introduction of new beliefs, regulations, and institutions, a good deal of the Islamic way consisted of a reform of existing customs and a continuance of that which was not in need of specific reform.

There are numerous ways in which custom became incorporated into Islamic law, among them, the procedures of the qadis (judges), the content of traditions (hadith), the Maliki regard for the ijma of Medina, and the fatwas of the muftis.

As noted previously, in the early courts of the Umayyad and early Abbasid periods, qadis would look to the Quran and Sunnah for guidance in rendering a decision, but in cases where no relevant texts were found, they would then resort to the custom of their community. An example from the sphere of family law is the division of dower (mahr). The practice was to separate the dower into two parts, the first paid immediately, and the other deferred usually until the end of the marriage. In situations in which the proportionate amounts had not been stipulated in the contract, the allotment was usually determined on the basis of local custom. This approach continued to be followed in modern times. The Majallah[57] (Ottoman

Civil Code) states: "A thing acknowledged by custom is regarded as an agreed upon stipulation" *(Article 43).*

A second avenue for the entrance of custom into Islamic law was the tradition *(hadith)* literature. The usual classification of the *Sunnah* is *al-sunnah al-qawliyah* (words), *al-sunnah al-filiyah* (deeds), and *al-sunnah al-taqririyah* (what Muhammad permitted). It is this last category, comprising actions performed in the presence of the Prophet without his disapproval, which represents that body of pre-Islamic Arabian customary practice that continued to be followed.

The *ijma* (consensus) of the Maliki law school, which was restricted to that of the Medinan community, is indicative of another historical source for custom. Where no explicit text existed, the customs of the Medinese were regarded as a legal source. Besides the importance of the Prophet's community, this Maliki concept reflects the early tendency for the *ijma* to be a local geographical consensus (e.g., the *ijma* of Kufa, Basra, Medina) that became the *sunnah,* or ideal pattern of behavior, of each local school. For example, the doctrine of marriage equality *(kafaah),* which required that the husband be the equal of his wife in a number of respects, among them lineage, financial standing, and profession, is most prominent in the Hanafi school and reflects the practice of a more socially stratified, class-conscious society than Medina.

A final source for the incorporation of custom in law was the *fatwas* (opinions) of *muftis* (legal consultants). A *fatwa* is an opinion on a point of law rendered by a *mufti* in response to a question submitted to him by a private individual or by a *qadi.* The need for the office of *mufti* existed from the earliest period of legal development. Due to the vast expansion of Islam, the Islamic community found itself mingling with new cultures, novel ideas, and new problems. There were myriad occasions necessitating reference to competent legal scholars. As law developed and became increasingly complex, these legal specialists became increasingly important. Where a specific revealed text did not provide an answer to the legal problem before them, *muftis* adopted or modified customs of the day in light of *Shariah* values. As the times and their customs changed, so too might the substance of the *fatwa.*

The function of the *mufti* was essentially private and consultative, and so a *fatwa* was not legally binding, although it could be utilized by a *qadi* and incorporated in his decision. More important, when a *fatwa* issued by a *mufti* on a new problem became recognized by the *ijma* of the scholars of a school, it was incorporated in the legal handbooks of the school. Finally, compilations of the responses of noted *muftis,* such as the *Fatawa Alamgiriyya,* came to be reckoned among the important authoritative legal references complimenting the standard *Shariah* manuals.

Although not officially recognized by classical theory, customary practice, then, came to form a substantial part of Islamic law. This realization should assist reformers in three ways. First, it underscores the extent to which custom did contribute to the body of substantive law, and so the inclusion of modern social standards or customs can be viewed as consistent with the manner in which law had been formulated to meet particular social needs in the past. Second, it demonstrates the process of Islamization of this customary law and therefore lays the foundation and provides the method for the replacing of old customs with newly Islamized customs appropriate to changed social situations. Third, it emphasizes the extent to which *fiqh* was influenced by fallible and mutable human understanding both in its content (since custom is the nonrevelational product of a human society) and method (the reason of the *qadis, muftis,* and jurists of the law schools whose decisions incorporated custom in law). This makes the distinction between *Shariah* and *fiqh* that much clearer to all who still do not distinguish the immutable and the sacrosanct in Islamic law from the fallible, the particular, and the human.

Conclusion

At the dawn of the twenty-first century, the challenges of modernization and change in the Muslim world remain, although significant progress has been made in both recognizing the need for reform and working toward it. Muslim family law remains the major arena for Islamic reform, requiring Muslims to grapple with two major issues: (1) the relationship between tradition and change, and (2) the means or methodology for reinterpretation and reform.

The classical theory of law presented a definitive picture of the formation of law, both its jurisprudential method *(usul al-fiqh)* and the branches of substantive law themselves *(furu al-fiqh)*. The four sources of law *(Quran, Sunnah, qiyas,* and *ijma)* produced a body of law consisting of religious observances *(ibadat)* and social transactions *(muamalat)* of which family law is a major part. Between the end of the tenth century and beginning of the twelfth century, the consensus *(ijma)* of scholars concluded that the basic rules of law had been discerned and the founding of new schools of Islamic law *(madhhabs)* ceased. In the Hanafi, Maliki and majority of Shafii schools, the exercise of *ijtihad* ended and the reign of *taqlid* (imitation) began. In these schools, down through the ages, with a few exceptions, the consensus of medieval jurists affirmed the completeness and authoritativeness for all times of law *(fiqh)* as found in the books of these schools, indicating that the law was complete and that there was no need for substantive change. Only the Hanbalis and a few Shafiis continued to assert the right to exercise *ijtihad*.

As long as the structure of Muslim society remained essentially unchanged, Islamic law could generally meet the needs of the times. This is especially evident in the area of family law, which remained operative until contemporary times. Muslim family law provided a well-developed, comprehensive approach to the major aspects of family life—marriage, divorce, inheritance, etc.—that was basically in tune with medieval Muslim society. Thus, during the long span of ten centuries, the classical view of law reigned throughout Muslim society.

However, this stable situation has been disrupted in the modern period as Muslim societies have sought to respond to the challenges of modernization. The results of these new developments have led to social changes, among them changes in family structure and, most especially, in woman's status and role in society. While these changes have not affected all of society to the same degree, reforms in Muslim family law have occurred in most Muslim countries.

Despite the changes thus far, the conflict between the forces of conservatism and modernism has continued. Resistance to change often resulted in indirect, *ad hoc* legal methods of reform as well as the shelving of draft legislation. The problem that has emerged is still very much that of *taqlid* (following tradition) versus *ijtihad* (reinterpretation), the infallibility of classical law versus legal change. The task is not easy, namely, to provide an Islamic rationale for change, one clearly rooted in Islamic history.

The importance of providing an Islamic methodology for Islamic reform is especially evident today. As noted at the outset of this study, one aspect of the Islamic renewal is a call for more Islamically oriented societies. Given the totality of Islam and the comprehensiveness of its worldview as reflected in Islamic law, this has meant a call for more *Shariah* law. Potentially, such change could affect every area of life, from the nature and institutions of the state to family relations. Debates on the advisability of such attempts, as well as the nature of a return to *Shariah* rule, have taken place from Egypt and the Sudan to Pakistan and Malaysia. Does a return to *Shariah* law mean simply going back to those laws that developed during the first centuries of Islam and reflect the society of those times, or will it be a law that is the product of reinterpretation *(ijtihad)* and reform? As Muslims seek to root their personal and national identity in an Islamic past, the importance of reinterpretation *(ijtihad)* and community consensus *(ijma)* is evident.

Providing an Islamic methodology for reform is an essential part of this process. Lack of such a methodology undermines any sense of the Islamic character of reforms and consequently the acceptance of such reforms by the vast majority of Muslims. Although passage of reforms may be effected through an autocratic leader of a legislature comprised of a small elite, their ultimate acceptance by the vast majority of the Islamic community will not be assured. Thus, for example, the Islamic Republic of Iran repealed the secular *Family Protection Act of 1967* due to its departure from classical Ithna 'Ashari law and its secular nature, replacing it with a new *Civil Code* that combined Ithna 'Ashari legal precepts with modern reformist tendencies. The new *Civil Code,* one of the most advanced marriage laws in the Middle East, is an important example of the tendency to adhere to classical legal precepts while at the same time recognizing and accommodating modern conditions. It is also noteworthy that many of the provisions of the *Civil Code* are similar to those of the *Family Protection Act,* but have been presented in a manner that reflects the regime's sensitivity to the need for an Islamic justification for such reforms. An important example is the standard insertion of certain stipulations in marriage contracts to ensure that every woman knows what she has a legal right to demand, but still requiring that the couple negotiate the implementation of those stipulations, thus maintaining the spirit of negotiation critical to the process of contracting marriage.

Similarly, Pakistan reviewed certain provisions of the *Muslim Family Laws Ordinance of 1961*, which was based upon a weak Islamic methodology. Since the implementation of an Islamization process begun by Zia ul-Haq in 1979, the *Shariah* has come to play a more prominent role in Pakistani legislation. Nevertheless, the debate over whether civil or Islamic law should prevail continues in Pakistan today because concerns have been raised about the relationship between classical interpretations of *Shariah* and modern principles of justice, democracy and women's rights.

In Egypt, the family law reforms of 1979 were ultimately overturned owing to the questionable Islamic methodology and means by which they were implemented. Although a revised version of the reforms was passed in 1985, it measures are less expansive than those of the preceding legislation, reflecting a stronger spirit of religious conservatism than existed in 1979. Therefore, care in choosing the mechanisms through which to render reforms is of the utmost importance. Islamic jurisprudence provides the resources for such an undertaking.

Contemporary scholarship has begun to provide the historical perspective and materials for such a project. The complex origins of Islamic law, long forgotten by the idealized traditional picture of classical theory, have resurfaced and, if properly interpreted, provide a historical justification for Muslim family law reform. More importantly, a new understanding of the law's development demonstrates that Islamic jurisprudence is fully capable of again providing the methods for reform.

To once more realize the divine imperative in history, the Muslim community possesses its immutable source—the *Quran*. Constant and firm belief that this source book of Islamic values is the very revealed word of God provides Muslims with the principles and values upon which to base legal reform. If *Quranic* values are applied correctly, Muslim society can accommodate social change in the twenty-first century while preserving its link with the history of the Islamic tradition. Furthermore, the task of reassessing the role of the *Sunnah* and its utilization in legal reform will not be a novel endeavor. Voices calling for a historical critique and re-evaluation of the *hadith* have existed throughout Islamic history, from the early movement that led to the development of the science of *hadith* criticism, to pre-modern reformers like Muhammad ibn Abd al-Wahhab and Shah Wali Allah, and finally to the Muslim modernists of the twentieth century.[58]

However, the successful implementation of the last two sources of legal reform *(ijtihad* and *ijma)* constitutes the greatest challenge for contemporary Muslim society. Education continues to be the most important ingredient for change, for Islamic reform in general and women's status in particular. The basic fight against illiteracy and the struggle to reform the educational systems of both secular and religious institutions are essential. An important task in educational reform is the implementation of measures which ensure that the educational system incorporates the best of both scientific knowledge and religious values.

Part of the legacy of modernity is the bifurcation of education in most Muslim countries through the creation of modern (national) schools alongside traditional Islamic schools *(madrasahs)*, each with a curriculum reflecting the differing and competing worldviews on which the systems were based.[59] The situation has been further compounded in those Muslim countries where the government sharply curtailed direct financial support for Islamic schools and reduced their revenue through the reform or repeal of religious endowments *(waqfs)*. The result of this bifurcation became apparent in the 1960s and 1970s. Western educated elites, possessed of modern scientific and technological skills but little intellectual knowledge of or appreciation for their tradition, lacked the vision to draft reforms that took into account the history and values of their culture. Traditionally educated individuals encountered a limited curriculum that provided neither a full appreciation of modern problems nor an intellectual outlook that incorporated a sense of the creative, dynamic process which characterized the formative period of Islam. Thus, they were less open to substantive reinterpretation and reform. As Fazlur Rahman observed regarding the traditional Islamic schools: "The *madrasa* have . . . aimed at merely

imparting a system of ideas not at creating newer systems; and therefore they have not been interested in inculcating the spirit of inquiry
and independent thought."[60]

This situation began to change in the 1980s and 1990s, as many
lay professionals, both men and women, began to insert themselves
into the debates about the role of Islam in modern, global society.
Doctors, engineers, professors, and lawyers, among others, have become active participants and leaders in the movements from Tunisia
to Malaysia that support the Islamic revival, serving as advisors to
governmental and judicial bodies seeking to Islamize various disciplines, as well as the law. Thus, it is evident that education is a key
factor in assuring the expertise necessary for a wise reinterpretation
(ijtihad) and an enlightened community consensus *(ijma)* that keeps
pace with social change.

Indeed, the Islamic revival has highlighted the existence of a
generation of lay professionals engaged in the task of Islamic reform. In general, these reformers are not members of the *ulama;*
many are Western-educated but Islamically oriented. Alongside the
Ayatollah Khomeini and the majority of Iranian religious leaders,
the Islamic movement in Iran has included others like the sociologist
Ali Shariati, and the economist and former Iranian president Abol
Hasan Bani Sadr, both Sorbonne educated.[61] The more vibrant leaders of the Islamic movement in Malaysia are Western-educated professors and students.[62] Likewise, among the leaders of the Islamic
movement in the Sudan are the Oxford-educated former prime minister, Sadiq al-Mahdi, and the London-Sorbonne educated president
of the Muslim Brotherhood Party, Hassan al-Turabi.

While differences abound, these Islamic reformers do share certain common attitudes. First, there is an acceptance of modernization, but a rejection of an uncritical adoption of westernization and
secularization. Second, there is general agreement that more indige-
nously (Islamically) oriented models of political, economic, and social change need to be implemented. Third, reformers claim the right
to *ijtihad* and thus reject a blind following of the past. Fourth, their
methodology includes a return to fundamentals (in this sense they
may truly be termed fundamentalists!), i.e., to the *Quran* and the
Sunnah of the Prophet. While reverencing past tradition, they do not
feel bound to it, since they view the traditional world view embod-

ied in Islamic law as the product of past *ijtihad* to meet historically conditioned needs. Therefore, they see themselves as undertaking once again the process of Islamization which characterized the early formative period of Islam—a process during which Muslims borrowed freely from other cultures, adopted and adapted the best that was available, and added their own distinctive contributions. Once again, reformers seek to interpret and apply Islamic principles and values to the exigencies of modern life and thus develop appropriate Islamically acceptable responses for modern Muslim societies.

The challenges facing the developing nations of the Islamic world are formidable. What path(s) Muslim countries will ultimately choose is an open-ended question. For many, a present and future that embody some continuity with their Islamic past will continue to be an important concern, not only for Muslim majority countries but also for Muslim minorities living in non-Muslim majority countries, such as India and the United States, as they seek ways of publicly expressing their religious beliefs in what are largely secular societies. Questions such as whether all Muslims living in a non-Muslim majority country should be governed by a single personal status law, who is to interpret that law, which law—civil or religious—is ultimately to prevail, how to ensure that obligations under religious law are carried out in countries ruled by secular law, and how to carry out true religious pluralism while maintaining national coherence, all remain challenges for the future. Likewise, the questions of how non-Muslims living in Muslim majority countries are to be considered under the law and whether they should be subject to a law that does not constitute part of their religious belief systems also remain challenges in an increasingly global and mobile society.

Given the traditional role of Islamic law as the ideal, comprehensive statement of the Islamic way of life, it is clear that calls for more *Shariah* reform to address modern conditions are inevitable. Cases in point are the quest for international standards for human rights and the elimination of discrimination on the basis of gender and religion. One means of ensuring just and lasting reforms, particularly with respect to family law, is the inclusion of women in the legal-ethical deliberations about women's rights and status both in the family and in society. Women also need to be educated about their legal rights and provided with support networks that enable them to assert the rights granted to them by law. The status changes stemming from Muslim women's increasing access to both educational and employment opportunities has already intensified the pressure for family law reforms that reflect modern socioeconomic realities and will continue to do so.

Islamic history, if correctly understood, has a lesson for both conservatives and reformers. It offers a picture of a dynamic, changing, adaptive religious tradition. A fuller appreciation of the real as well as the idealized Islamic past can provide the understanding and means or methodology on which to base Islamic responses to the challenge of modernity as Muslims once more repeat the process of Islamization—to develop a viable political, legal, and economic model for society and to draw on all available data and practices, but to do so in light of *Quranic* principles and values.

Notes

Modern Legal Codes Consulted

Suggested Readings

Index

.

Notes

1—The Sources of Islamic Law

1. "[He is] Creator of the heavens and the earth. When He decrees a thing, he only says to it: 'Be,' and there it is." (2:116); see also 7:54 and 31:10. All Quranic references are from Majid Fakhry, trans. The Qur'an: A Modern English Version. Reading, England: Garnet Publishing Limited, 1997.

2. The scope of this study is restricted to Sunni Islam, that branch of Islam which encompasses 90 percent of the world's Muslims.

3. Shihab al-Din al-Qarafi, Adh Dhakhira (Cairo: n.p., 1961) 1:119. See also Muhammad ibn Idris al-Shafii Al-Risala fi usul al-fiqh (Cairo: Bulak, 1321 A.H.), 65–66.

4. N. J. Coulson, A History of Islamic Law (Edinburgh: Univ. of Edinburgh Press, 1964), 40.

5. Reuben Levy, The Social Structure of Islam (Cambridge: Cambridge Univ. Press, 1971), 127.

2—Classical Muslim Family Law

1. See also Quran 6:151 and 17:31.

2. Charles Hamilton, trans., The Hedaya (Lahore: Premier Book House, 1957), 37.

3. Sir D. F. Mulla, Principles of Mahomedan Law, 16th ed. (Bombay: Tripathi, 1968), 263.

4. See Hamudab Abd al-Ati, The Family Structure in Islam (Ann Arbor: University Microfilm, 1971), 253–60, for a discussion of the religious, sociological, and psychological reasons for this prohibition.

5. How high soever (h.h.s.) and how low soever (h.l.s.) refer to continuing the same family line as far as conceivable. For example, a son h.l.s. can refer to a son's son's son's son. A grandfather h.h.s. can refer to a father's father's father's father.

6. Neil B. E. Baillie, A Digest of Moohummudan Law, 4th ed. (Lahore: Premier Book House, 1965), 35.

7. Seymour Vesey-Fitzgerald, Muhammadan Law: An Abridgement (London: Oxford Univ. Press, 1931), 96–98.

8. Coulson, *History of Islamic Law,* 175.

9. Faiz Badruddin Tyabji, *Muhammadan Law: The Personal Law of Muslims,* 3d ed. (Bombay: Tripathi, 1940), 264–65.

10. Hamilton, *The Hedaya,* 73.

11. See, for example, *Quran* 65:1.

12. Vesey-Fitzgerald, *Muhammadan Law,* 73.

13. Two other forms of divorce initiated by the husband are very rare: *ila* and *zihar.* In the case of *ila,* or Vow of Continence, the husband vows not to have intercourse with his wife, and if he abstains for four months, in Hanafi law, the marriage is dissolved without legal process. However, he may revoke the vow by merely resuming marital life.

Zihar, derived from *zahr* (back), is an archaic form of an oath coming from pre-Islamic Arabia that means "to oppose back to back." To represent dissension between husband and wife, the spouses turn their backs on the other partner. In the language of law, *zihar* signifies a husband comparing his wife to a female relative within the prohibited degrees of kinship. *Zihar* by itself does not dissolve the marriage. After the husband has taken this oath, his wife has the right to file for restitution of conjugal rights.

14. See chap. 3, p. 79.

15. Tyabji, *Muhammadan Law,* 275–76.

16. For additional information, see Baillie, *Digest,* 696–700; Tyabji, *Muhammadan Law,* 839, 843–60; Mulla, *Principles,* 58–62; N. J. Coulson, *Succession in the Muslim Family* (Cambridge: Cambridge Univ. Press, 1971), 40–46.

17. *The Sirajiyyah* by Siraju al-din Md. b. Abdu al-Rashid al-Sajawandi is the highest authority on inheritance among the Hanafis.

18. *Sirajiyyah,* 23–24, as cited in A. A. A. Fyzee, *Outlines of Muhammadan Law,* 3d ed. (London: Oxford Univ. Press, 1964), 411.

19. See also *Quran* 2:240, which prescribes that a testator bequeath one year's maintenance with residence to his widow.

20. See chap. 3, p. 64.

21. *Mishkat al-Masabih* (Lahore: Sh. Muhammad Ashraf, 1973) 12:xx, 1.

22. *Ibid.* 12:xx, 2.

23. Baillie, *Digest,* 557.

3—Modern Muslim Family Law in Comparative Perspective

1. *Commercial Code of 1850, Penal Code of 1858, Code of Commercial Procedure of 1861,* and *Code of Maritime Commerce of 1863.*

2. Although the majority of Egyptians were followers of the Shafii school, the Hanafi school has been the authoritative source of the courts since the sixteenth century, when the Ottoman Empire established it as the official law school. This action was reaffirmed by *Article 280 of Shariah Courts Organization Regulations, 1910,* in which predominant opinions of the Hanafi school were officially endorsed.

3. *Al-Manar,* 35 vols. (Cairo: Manar Press, 1912) 12:331.

4. Muhammad Abduh and Muhammad Rashid Rida, *Tafsir al-Qur'an al-Hakim,* 12 vols. (Cairo: Manar Press, 1349/1930) 4:349 ff.

5. Qasim Amin, *Tahrir al-Mar'ah* (Cairo: n.p., 1899), 165, 184.

6. Quoted in C. C. Adams, *Islam and Modernism in Egypt* (Oxford: Oxford Univ. Press, 1933), 231.

7. J. N. D. Anderson, "Recent Developments in Shariah Law III," *Muslim World* 41 (1951): 113.

8. See chap. 2, p. 34.

9. See chap. 2, p. 16.

10. See chap. 2, p. 35.

11. This provision requiring payment of past maintenance was the cause of many false claims as to the arrears date. The *Code of 1931* decreed that claims could not be in excess of three years prior to the date of the suit.

12. *Articles 15 and 17, Law No. 25, 1929.*

13. See chap. 2, pp. 35–36.

14. Although the other Sunni schools of law do not allow dissolution of marriage, they each recommend other methods for handling cases of maltreatment.

15. *Article 9, Law No. 25, 1929.* While this legislation is principally of Maliki origin, one significant difference exists. Whereas the Maliki school allows for a *khul* divorce when the wife is judged at fault, the reform legislation makes no provision for divorce in such cases.

16. See chap. 2, p. 34.

17. The law here differs from traditional Maliki law only in its recognition of valid excuses for separation such as business or study, a position followed by the Hanbali school.

18. In fact, the original intent of this law was to discourage a lighthearted or frivolous treatment of divorce and underscore the seriousness of a repudiation; nevertheless, hardship and injustice often occurred when an "unintended" divorce occurred as a result of a repudiation uttered under compulsion or in a state of intoxication.

19. *Article 4, Law No. 25, 1929.* Inexplicably, formulae uttered in jest were not included.

20. See chap. 2, p. 31.

21. Some legal scholars, such as Ibn Taymiyya, condemned *tahlil* as an abuse of the spirit of the law and thus invalid.

22. *Al-Ahram,* June 7, 1971.

23. *Ibid.,* Feb. 8, 1971.

24. *Ibid.,* Dec. 23, 1971.

25. *Ibid.,* Dec. 27, 1971.

26. *Articles 76–79, Law of Testamentary Dispositions of 1946.*

27. The general limitation for testamentary dispositions is one-third of the testator's estate.

28. See pp. 49–50.

29. *Article 30, Egyptian Code of Procedure for Shariah Courts, 1897.*

30. *Explanatory Memorandum, Law of Rules Relevant to Waqf of 1946.*

31. However, it is noteworthy that the law did not (as it does for obligatory bequests) oblige the founder to grant the entitlement to his orphaned grandchildren.

32. Since the Indian subcontinent was a single entity prior to the partitioning of 1947 and because the legal system of Pakistan incorporated the Indian legal tradition (its laws and case history) the term India-Pakistan is used when referring to the region in the period prior to 1947.

33. I. H. Qureshi, *The Muslim Community of the Indo-Pakistan Subcontinent (610–1947)* (The Hague: Mouton, 1961), 212.

34. Aziz Ahmad, *Islamic Modernism in India and Pakistan 1857–1964* (New York: Oxford Univ. Press, 1967), 27.

35. As quoted in B. A. Dar, *Religious Thought of Sayyid Ahmad Khan* (Lahore: Muhammad Ashraf, 1957), 7.

36. Ahmad Khan, *Majmu'a Lectures* as quoted in Dar, *Religious Thought,* 139.

37. *Tafsir al-Qur'an* (Lahore: n.p., 1880–95); *al-Tahrir fi usul al-tafsir* (Lahore: n.p., 1892), and others.

38. Ahmad, *Islamic Modernism,* 74–76.

39. Chiragh Ali, *The Proposed Political, Legal and Social Reforms in the Ottoman Empire and Other Mohammedan States* (Bombay, n.p., 1883), 64.

40. *Ibid.,* 118.

41. *Ibid.,* 112–13.

42. *The Egyptian Law of Inheritance of 1943* cites 270 days as its limit; see 136.

43. *Section 2A, Child Marriage Restraint Act, 1929.*

44. *Sections 4 and 6* were amended by *Sections 12–13* of the *Muslim Family Law Ordinance of 1961,* which reduced the minimum age for males from twenty-one to eighteen years of age.

45. Preamble to *The Dissolution of Muslim Marriages Act, 1939.*

46. *Gazette of India* Part V (1938), 36.

47. See chap. 2, p. 16.

48. This regulation was changed to sixteen years of age by the *Muslim Family Laws Ordinance of 1961.*

49. *Section 2.7, The Dissolution of Muslim Marriages Act, 1939.*

50. See p. 55.

51. *Section 2.6, The Dissolution of Muslim Marriages Act, 1939.* Other chronic or dangerous diseases have been included in judicial interpretations.

52. See pp. 54–55.

53. *Pakistan Legal Decision,* 1952 (W.P.) Lahore 113 (F.B.). Hereafter cited as *PLD.*

54. *PLD* 1952 (W.P.) Lahore 113 (F.B.).

55. See chap. 2, p. 32.

56. *PLD* 1959 (W.P.) Lahore 566 (paragraph 42).

57. *PLD* 1959 (W.P.) Lahore 566.

58. See p. 50.

59. Section 13 of this ordinance is entitled "Amendment of the *Dissolution of Muslim Marriages Act, 1939* (VIII, 1939)," and directs that the following amendment be added to Section II regarding grounds for divorce: "(iia) that the husband has

taken an additional wife in contravention of the provisions of the *Muslim Family Laws Ordinance, 1961.*"

60. See p. 54.

61. *APWA Recommendation on Family Laws Ordinance* (Lahore: n.p.).

62. Preamble to *The West Pakistan Family Courts Act, 1964* (Act XXV of 1964).

63. *Gul Newaz Khan v. Maherunnessa Begum* 3 PLD, 1965 (E.P.) Dacca 274, 276.

64. *Report of the Commission for Eradication of Social Evils* (Government of Pakistan Ministry of Health, Labour and Social Welfare, 1965) #17.

65. Fyzee, *Outlines of Muhammadan Law,* 293–94.

66. *Act No. VI (Mussalman Waqf Validating Act, 1913, Section 4).*

67. A similar defense can be found in Kemal Faruki, *Islamic Studies* 4, no.3 (1965): 264 ff.

68. The courts had taken this position repeatedly. See, for example, *Aga Mahomed v. Koolson Beebe* (1897) and *Baker Ali Khan v. Anjuman Ara Begum* (1903) 30 *India Appeals* 94.

69. *Sayeeda Khanum v. Muhammad Sami* (1950) PLD 113.

70. N. J. Coulson, *Conflicts and Tensions in Islamic Jurisprudence* (Chicago: Univ. of Chicago Press, 1969), 106–7.

71. *Ibid.,* 111–12.

4—Toward a Legal Methodology for Reform

1. See pp. 124–26.

2. Subhi Mahmasani, *Falsafat al-Tashri fi al-Islam* translated by Farhat J. Ziadeh (Leiden: E.J. Brill, 1961), 39.

3. For a more detailed discussion of this subject, see Wael Hallaq, "Was the Gate of Ijtihad Closed?" *International Journal of Middle East Studies* 16, no. 1 (1983): 3–41; "On the Origins of the Controversy about the Existence of Mujtahids and the Gate of Ijtihad" *Studia Islamica* 63 (1986): 129–41; and *A History of Islamic Legal Theories: An introduction to Sunni usul al-fiqh* (New York: Cambridge Univ. Press, 1997).

4. Muhammad Abduh, *The Theology of Unity, (Risalat* al-Tauhid) translated by Ishaq Musaad and Kenneth Cragg (London: George Allen and Unwin, 1966), 66.

5. *Ibid.,* 39–40.

6. Muhammad Iqbal, *The Reconstruction of Religious Thought in Islam* (rpt. Lahore: Sh. Muhammad Ashraf, 1934), 178.

7. Ismail Ragi al-Faruqi, "Towards a New Methodology of Qur'anic Exegesis," *Islamic Studies* (March 1962), 35.

8. See, for example, *ibid.,*35–52; also Subhi Mahmasani, "Muslims: Decadence and Renaissance," *Muslim World* 44 (1954): 192–93 and *Falsafat al-Tashri,* 109.

9. Al-Faruqi, "Towards a New Methodology for Qur'anic Exegesis," *Islamic Studies* (March 1962), 36–37.

10. Coulson, *A History of Islamic Law,* 225.

11. See, for example, Ismail Ragi al-Faruqi, *On Arabism, Urubah and Religion* (Amsterdam: Djambatan, 1962), 175–76. See especially Al-Faruqi's "Towards a New Methodology for *Quranic* Exegesis," *Islamic Studies* (March 1962), 35–52, in which the need and value foundations for this approach are explored.

12. See also *Quran* 3:195; 4:32; 4:124; 5:41; 24:2; 28:6, et al.

13. See, for example, Gustav E. von Grunebaum, *Medieval Islam* (Chicago: Univ. of Chicago Press, 1946), 174–75; A. A. A. Fyzee, *A Modern Approach to Islam* (Bombay: Asia Publishing House, 1963), 103.

14. For a contemporary Muslim reinterpretation based upon a new grammatical and contextual analysis, see Abd al-Ati, *The Family Structure in Islam*, 298 ff, especially 309–16.

15. As cited in Muhammad Abdul-Rauf, *Marriage in Islam* (New York: Exposition Press, 1972), 14.

16. As cited in M. Mazheruddin Siddiqi, *Women In Islam* (Lahore: Institute of Islamic Culture, 1971), 60.

17. *Ibid.*, 80.

18. See chap. 2, p. 19.

19. See chap. 3, pp. 48, 72.

20. For further development of this line of thought, see Amina Wadud, *Quran and Woman: Rereading the Sacred Text from a Woman's Perspective* 2d ed. (New York: Oxford Univ. Press, 1999).

21. Mahmasani, "Muslims: Decadence and Renaissance," 199.

22. See chap. 1, pp. [X-REF 000].

23. I. Goldziher, *Le dogme et la loi de l'Islam*, translated by F. Arin (Paris: Paul Geuthner, 1920); D. S. Margoliouth, *The Early Development of Mohammedanism* (London: Williams and Norgate, 1914), 65–98; C. Snouck Hurgronje, *Selected Works of C. Snouck Hurgronje*, edited by C. H. Bousquet and Joseph Schacht, (Leiden: Brill, 1957).

24. The significance of Schacht's views lies in the fact that he is considered by many to be the most influential Orientalist in the field of Islamic law in the twentieth century. He has deeply influenced Western scholarship through his long teaching career and his many publications on Islamic law, including the pioneering works, *Origins of Muhammadan Jurisprudence* (Oxford: Oxford Univ. Press, 1950) and *Introduction to Islamic Law* (Oxford: Oxford Univ. Press, 1966).

25. Joseph Schacht, *Origins of Muhammadan Jurisprudence*, 138–76.

26. *Ibid.*, 140.

27. Tarif Khalidi, *Arabic Historical Thought in the Classical Period* (New York: Cambridge Univ. Press, 1994), 20.

28. Fazlur Rahman, "Sunna and Hadith," *Islamic Studies* 1 (June 1962): 4.

29. Khalidi, 22.

30. *Ibid.*, 21.

31. Rahman, "Concepts of Sunnah, Ijtihad and Ijma in the Early Period," *Islamic Studies* 1 (1962): 5.

32. Goldziher, *Muslim Studies* (London: George Allen and Unwin, 1971) 2:56.

33. Rahman, "Sunnah and Hadith," *Islamic Studies* 1 (June 1962): 13.

34. *Ibid.,* 31.

35. H. A. R. Gibb, *Mohammedanism* (New York: Oxford Univ. Press, 1952), 86.

36. In later terminology, *ray* came to mean arbitrary or personal opinion in contradistinction to the more disciplined *qiyas.*

37. Kemal Faruki, *Islamic Jurisprudence* (Karachi: Pakistan Publishing House, 1962), 147.

38. See, for example, *Quran* 4:29 and 16:90.

39. See, for example, *Quran* 4:58; 7:29; and 57:25.

40. See chap. 1, pp. 8–9.

41. See, for example, Muhammah Rashid Rida, ed., *Al-Manar,* 35 vols. (Cairo: Dar al-Manar, 1898–1935), 4:858–60; and Rida, *Yusr al-Islam wa Usul al-Tashri al-Amm* (Cairo: Dar al-Manar, 1928), 73 ff.

42. Chap. 3, p. 81.

43. Chap. 3, pp. 64–65.

44. See, for example, *Quran* 3:220; 4:2, 6, 10, 127; 17:34.

45. Chap. 2, pp. 37–38.

46. Chap. 3, p. 62.

47. Rida, *Al-Manar,* 5:181–82.

48. J. Jomier, *Le commentaire coranique du manar* (Paris: Maisonneuve, 1954), 193.

49. See Fazlur Rahman, *Islam* (New York: Doubleday, 1968), 83–84 and Kemal Faruki, *Islamic Jurisprudence,* 67 ff, and especially 156.

50. Ameer Ali, *The Spirit of Islam* (London: Oxford Univ. Press, 1922), 251, 278–79.

51. Iqbal, *Religious Thought in Islam,* 173.

52. *Ibid.,* 174.

53. Fazlur Rahman, "The Islamic Concept of State," in *Islam in Transition: Muslim Perspectives,* edited by John J. Donohue and John L. Esposito (New York: Oxford Univ. Press, 1982), 268.

54. *Ibid.*

55. Ali Shariati, "Intizar: The Religion of Protest" in Donohue and Esposito, *Islam in Transition,* 647. See also Rahman, "The Islamic Concept of State," 528; Kemal Faruki, *Islamic Jurisprudence,* 87, 163–64; Hassan Hanafi, "Religion and Revolution: An Islamic Model" in *Religious Dialogue and Revolution* (Cairo: The Anglo-Egyptian Bookshop, 1977), 205–6.

56. Although customary practice and its Islamization may be treated within the section on *ijtihad,* for the sake of clarity, separate consideration is necessary.

57. The *Majallah* (Majallah al-Ahkam-i-Adiya) was entirely derived from Hanafi law and codified between 1869 and 1876 for use in courts of the Ottoman Empire.

58. See, for example, the discussion by Abd al-Jalil Shalabi (a former secretary general of the Islamic Research Institute) in "Personal Status Laws in Opposition with Fiqh Texts" (Qanun al-ahwal al-shakhsiyah fi muwajahat al-nusus al-fiqhiyah), *al-Dawah,* 28, no. 41 (1979): 17–19.

59. See Cheikh Hamidou Kane, *Ambiguous Adventure* (New York: Collier Books, 1969), for a striking fictional presentation of this problem.

60. Rahman, "The Islamic Concept of State," 312.

61. See Mangol Bayat, "Islam in Pahlavi and Post-Pahlavi Iran: A Cultural Revolution?" in Esposito, *Islam and Development*, especially 98 ff.

62. See Fred R. von der Mehden, "Islamic Resurgence in Malaysia" in Esposito, *Islam and Development*, 169–70, 173–75.

Modern Legal Codes Consulted

Algeria—*Law No. 84–11 of 1984.*

Bangladesh—*Muslim Family Laws Ordinance of 1961.*

Egypt—*Law No. 25 of 1920; Law No. 25 of 1929; Law of Inheritance of 1943; Law of Testamentary Dispositions of 1946; Law of Rules Relevant to Waqf of 1946; Law No. 44 of 1979; Law No. 100 of 1985 Concerning the Provisions on Maintenance and Certain Matters of Personal Status; March 2000 Law Concerning Divorce.*

India—*Special Marriage Act of 1954; Dowry Prohibition Act of 1961; Criminal Procedure Code of 1973; Marriage Laws (Amendment) Act of 1976; Muslim Women (Protection of Rights on Divorce) Act of 1986; Bill No. 83 of 1988.*

Iran—*Family Protection Law of 1967; Special Civil Court Act of 1980; Civil Code of 1980.*

Iraq—*Law No. 188 of 1959; Law No. 11 of 1963; Law No. 21 of 1978.*

Jordan—*Law of the Rights of the Family No. 26 of 1947; Law of Personal Status No. 61 of 1976.*

Kuwait—*Law No. 51 of 1984.*

Lebanon—*Law of the Rights of the Family of 1962.*

Libya—*Law No. 10 of 1984.*

Modern Legal Codes Consulted

Malaysia—*Islamic Family Law Act; Shariah Court Enactment; Shariah Criminal Procedure Code; Shariah Civil Procedure Code of 1983.*

Morocco—*Personal Status Code of 1957–58.*

Pakistan—*Muslim Personal Law of Shariat of 1948; West Pakistan Land Reform Regulation of 1959; Muslim Family Laws Ordinance of 1961; West Pakistan Family Courts Act of 1964; West Pakistan Dowry (Prohibition on Display) Act of 1967; Dowry and Bridal Gifts (Restriction) Act of 1976; Hudood Ordinances of 1979; Qanun-e Shahadat Order of the Islamic Rules of Evidence Law of 1984; Ordinance XX of 1984; Enforcement of Shariah Ordinance of 1988.*

Somalia—*Family Law, Law No. 23 of 1975.*

Syria—*Personal Status Act of 1953; Law No. 34 of Personal Status of 1975.*

Tunisia—*Personal Status Law of 1956* (and amendments of 1962, 1964, 1966 and 1981).

Yemen—*Personal Status Law, Law No. 20 of 1992.*

Suggested Readings

Abbot, Freeland. *Islam and Pakistan*. Ithaca, N.Y.: Cornell Univ. Press, 1968.

Afkhami, Mahnaz, ed. *Faith & Freedom: Women's Human Rights in the Muslim World*. Syracuse: Syracuse Univ. Press, 1995.

Aghnides, N. P. *Mohammedan Theories of Finance*. New York: Columbia Univ. Press, 1916.

Ahmad, Aziz. *Islamic Modernism in India and Pakistan 1857–1964*. New York: Oxford Univ. Press, 1967.

Ahmad, K. N. *The Muslim Law of Divorce*. Islamabad: Islamic Research Institute, 1972.

Ahmad, Khurshid. *Marriage Commission Report X-Rayed*. Karachi: Charagh-i-Rah Publications, 1959.

Ahmed, Leila. *Women and Gender in Islam*. New Haven, Conn.: Yale Univ. Press, 1992.

Ali, Sayyid Ameer. *Law of Family Courts*. Karachi: Pakistan Law House, 1975.

———. *Mohammedan Law*. 6th ed. 2 vols. Lahore: All Pakistan Legal Decisions Publ., 1965.

Anderson, J. N. D. *Islamic Law in Africa*. London: Her Majesty's Stationery Office, 1954.

———. *Islamic Law in the Modern World*. New York: New York Univ. Press, 1959.

———. *Law Reform in the Muslim World*. London: Athlone, 1976.

An-Na'im, Abdullahi Ahmed. *Toward an Islamic Reformation: Civil Liberties, Human Rights, and International Law*. Syracuse: Syracuse Univ. Press, 1990.

Baer, Gabriel. *Population and Society in the Arab World*. London: Routledge and Kegan Paul, 1963.

Baillie, Neil B. E., trans. *A Digest of Moohummudan Law*. 4th ed. Lahore: Premier Book House, 1965.

Beck, Lois G., and Nikki Keddie, eds. *Women in the Muslim World.* Cambridge: Harvard Univ. Press, 1978.

de Bellefonds, Y. L. *Traité de Droit Musulman Comparé.* Paris: Mouton, 1965.

Berger, Morroe. *The Arab World Today.* New York: Doubleday, 1962.

Bodman, Herbert L. and Nayereh Tohidi, eds. *Women in Muslim Societies: Diversity Within Unity.* Boulder: Lynne Rienner Publishers, 1998.

Coulson, N. J. *A History of Islamic Law.* Edinburgh: Edinburgh Univ. Press, 1964; rpt. 1978.

———. *Conflicts and Tensions in Islamic Jurisprudence.* Chicago: Univ. of Chicago Press, 1969.

———. *Succession in the Muslim Family.* Cambridge: Cambridge Univ. Press, 1971.

Dahl, Tove Stang. *The Muslim Family: A Study of Women's Rights in Islam.* Translated by Ronald Walford. Oslo: Scandinavian Univ. Press, 1997.

Dennerlein, Bettina. "Changing Conceptions of Marriage in Algerian Personal Status Law." In *Perspectives on Islamic Law, Justice, and Society.* Edited by R. S. Khare, Lanham, Md.: Rowman & Littlefield Publishers, Inc., 1999.

Derrett, J. D. M. *Religion, Law and the State in India.* London: The Free Press, 1968.

Donohue, John J., and John L. Esposito, eds. *Islam in Transition.* New York: Oxford Univ. Press, 1981.

El Alami, Dawoud Sudqi and Doreen Hinchcliffe. *Islamic Marriage and Divorce Laws of the Arab World.* London: Kluwer Law International, 1996.

Elbendary, Amina. "Conditional Surrenders," *Al-Ahram Weekly.* 464 (January 2000): 13–19.

Esposito, John L., ed. *Islam and Development: Religion and Sociopolitical Change.* Syracuse: Syracuse Univ. Press, 1980.

———, ed. *The Oxford Encyclopedia of the Modern Islamic World.* 4 vols. New York: Oxford Univ. Press, 1995.

———, ed. *The Oxford History of Islam.* New York: Oxford Univ. Press, 2000.

Esposito, John L. and Yvonne Yazbeck Haddad, eds. *Islam, Gender and Social Change.* New York: Oxford Univ. Press, 1998.

Fakhry, Majid, trans. *The Qur'an: A Modern English Version.* Reading, England: Garnet Publishing Limited, 1997.

al-Faruqi, Ismail Ragi. *On Arabism, Urubah and Religion.* Amsterdam: Djambatan, 1962.

Faruki, K. A. *Islamic Jurisprudence*. Karachi: Pakistan Publishing House, 1962.

Fernea, Elizabeth W. and Basima Bezirgan. *Middle Eastern Muslim Women Speak*. Austin: Univ. of Texas Press, 1977.

Fyzee, A. A. A. *A Modern Approach to Islam*. Bombay: Asia Publishing House, 1963.

———. *Cases in the Muhammadan Law of India and Pakistan*. Oxford: Clarendon Press, 1965.

———. *Outlines of Muhammadan Law*. 4th ed. Oxford: Oxford Univ. Press, 1974.

Gibb, H. A. R. *Mohammedanism*. New York: Oxford Univ. Press, 1952.

Goldziher, Ignaz. *Muslim Studies*. Vol. 1. Albany: SUNY Press, 1967. Vol. 2. Albany: SUNY Press, 1972.

Haeri, Shahla. "Divorce in Contemporary Iran: A Male Prerogative in Self-Will." In *Islamic Family Law*. Edited by Chibli Mallat and Jane Connors. London: Graham & Trotman, 1990.

Hallaq, Wael. "Was the Gate of Ijtihad Closed?" *International Journal of Middle East Studies* 16, no. 1 (1984): 3–41.

———. "On the Origins of the Controversy about the Existence of Mujtahids and the Gate of Ijtihad," *Studia Islamica* 63 (1986): 129–41.

———. *A History of Islamic Legal Theories: An introduction to Sunni usul al-fiqh*. New York: Cambridge Univ. Press, 1997.

Hamady, Sonia. *Temperament and Character of the Arabs*. New York: Twayne, 1960.

Hamilton, Charles, trans. *The Hedaya*. 2d ed. Lahore: Premier Book House, 1957.

Hannan, Shah Abdul. *Social Laws of Islam*. Dhaka, Bangladesh: Bangladesh Institute of Islamic Thought (BIIT), 1995.

Hassa, Fayza. "A Matter of Mistrust," *Al-Ahram Weekly* 464 (January 2000): 13–19.

Hassan, Sharifah Zaleha Syed and Sven Cederroth. *Managing Marital Disputes in Malaysia: Islamic Mediators and Conflict Resolution in the Syariah Courts*. Richmond, Surrey, England: Curzon Press, Ltd., 1997.

Hoodfar, Homa. "Population Policy and Gender Equity in Post-Revolutionary Iran. In *Family, Gender, and Population in the Middle East: Policies in Context*. Edited by Carla Makhlouf Obermeyer. Cairo: The American Univ. in Cairo Press, 1995.

Hourani, A. H. *Arabic Thought in the Liberal Age*. Oxford: Oxford Univ. Press, 1969.

Hurgronje, C. Snouck. *Selected Works of . . .* Edited by C. H. Bousquet and Joseph Schacht. Leiden: Brill, 1957.

Iqbal, Muhammad. *The Reconstruction of Religious Thought in Islam.* Lahore: Sh. Muhammad Ashraf, rpt. 1971.

Kastoryano, Riva. "Muslim Migrants in France and Germany: Law and Policy in Family and Group Identity." In *Islamic Family Law.* Edited by Chibli Mallat and Jane Connors. London: Graham & Trotman, 1990.

Keddie, Nikki R. and Beth Baron, eds. *Women in Middle Eastern History: Shifting Boundaries in Sex and Gender.* New Haven, Conn.: Yale Univ. Press, 1991.

Kerr, Malcolm. *Islamic Reform.* Berkeley: Univ. of California Press, 1966.

Khadduri, M. *Islamic Jurisprudence.* Baltimore: Johns Hopkins Univ. Press, 1961.

———— and H. J. Liebesny *Law in the Middle East.* Washington, D.C.: Middle East Institute, 1955.

Khalid, Khalid M. *From Here We Start.* Translated by Ismail R. al-Faruqi. Washington, D.C.: American Council of Learned Societies, 1953.

Khalidi, Tarif. *Arabic Historical Thought in the Classical Period.* New York: Cambridge Univ. Press, 1994.

Khare, R. S. *Perspectives on Islamic Law, Justice, and Society.* Lanham, Md.: Rowman & Littlefield Publishers, Inc., 1999.

Levy, R. *The Social Structure of Islam.* Cambridge: Cambridge Univ. Press, 1957.

Liebesny, H. J. *The Law of the Near and Middle East.* Albany: SUNY Press, 1975.

Macdonald, D. B. *Development of Muslim Theology, Jurisprudence and Constitutional Theory.* Lahore: Premier Book House, 1964.

Mahmasani, Subhi. *Falsafat al-Tashri fi al-Islam. (The Philosophy of Jurisprudence in Islam)* Translated by Farhat J. Ziadeh. Leiden: Brill, 1961.

Mahmood, Shaukat. *Principles and Digest of Muslim Law.* Lahore: Pakistan Law Times Publications, 1967.

Mahmood, Tahir. *Family Law Reform in the Muslim World.* New Delhi: N. M. Tripathi, 1972.

Mahmood, Tahir. "Islamic Family Law: Latest Developments in India." In *Islamic Family Law.* Edited by Chibli Mallat and Jane Connors. London: Graham & Trotman, 1990.

Mallat, Chibli. "Introduction—Islamic Family Law: Variations on State Identity and Community Rights." In *Islamic Family Law.* Edited by Chibli Mallat and Jane Connors. London: Graham & Trotman, 1990.

————. "Shi'ism and Sunnism in Iraq: Revisiting the Codes." In *Islamic Family Law.* Edited by Chibli Mallat and Jane Connors. London: Graham & Trotman, 1990.

———— and Jane Connors, eds. *Islamic Family Law.* London: Graham & Trotman, 1990.

Maududi, A. A. *Islamic Law and Its Introduction in Pakistan.* Karachi: Charagh-i-Rah, 1955.

Mehdi, Rubya. *The Islamization of the Law in Pakistan.* Richmond, Surrey, England: Curzon, 1994.

Menski, Werner F. "The Reform of Islamic Family Law and a Uniform Civil Code for India." In *Islamic Family Law.* Edited by Chibli Mallat and Jane Connors. London: Graham & Trotman, 1990.

Merchant, M. V. *Quranic Laws.* Lahore: Sh. Muhammad Ashraf, 1947.

Mernissi, Fatima. *Beyond the Veil.* Cambridge: Schenkman, 1975.

Mir-Hosseini, Ziba. *Marriage on Trial: A Study of Islamic Family Law. Iran and Morocco Compared.* London: I.B. Tauris & Co., Ltd., 1993.

Mitri, Tarek, ed. *Religion, Law and Society: A Christian-Muslim Discussion.* Geneva: World Council of Churches Publications, 1995.

Mulla, D. F. *Principles of Mahomedan Law.* Bombay: N. M. Tripathi, 1976.

Nasir, Jamal J. *The Islamic Law of Personal Status.* Arab & Islamic Law Series. 2d ed. London: Graham & Trotman, 1990.

————. *The Status of Women Under Islamic Law and Under Modern Islamic Legislation.* Boston & London: Graham & Trotman, 1990.

Obermeyer, Carla Makhlouf, ed. *Family, Gender, and Population in the Middle East: Policies in Context.* Cairo: The American Univ. in Cairo Press, 1995.

————. "Reproductive Rights in the West and in the Middle East: A Cross-Cultural Perspective." In *Family, Gender, and Population in the Middle East: Policies in Context.* Edited by Carla Makhlouf Obermeyer. Cairo: The American Univ. in Cairo Press, 1995.

Ostrorog, Count Leon. *The Angora Reform.* London, n.p., 1927.

Pearl, David. *A Textbook of Muslim Law.* London: Croom Helm, 1979.

————. "Three Decades of Executive, Legislative and Judicial Amendments to Islamic Family Law in Pakistan." In *Islamic Family Law.* Edited by Chibli Mallat and Jane Connors. London: Graham & Trotman, 1990.

Poulter, Sebastian. "The Claim to a Separate Islamic System of Personal Law for British Muslims." In *Islamic Family Law.* Edited by Chibli Mallat and Jane Connors. London: Graham & Trotman, 1990.

Rahman, Fazlur. *Islam.* New York: Doubleday, 1968.

Ramadan, Said. *Islamic Law: Its Scope and Equity.* London: Macmillan, 1970.

Roberts, Robert. *The Social Laws of the Quran.* London: Oxford Univ. Press, 1925.

Sachedina, Abdulaziz. "Woman, Half-the-Man? Crisis of Male Epistemology in Islamic Jurisprudence." In *Perspectives on Islamic Law, Justice, and Society*. Edited by R. S. Khare. Lanham, Md.: Rowman & Littlefield Publishers, Inc., 1999.

Sachs, Susan. "Egypt's Women Win Equal Rights to Divorce," *The New York Times*. March 1, 2000.

Schacht, Joseph. *The Origins of Muhammadan Jurisprudence*. Oxford: Clarendon Press, 1950.

———. *An Introduction to Islamic Law*. Oxford: Clarendon Press, 1964.

Shehadeh, Lamia Rustum. "The Legal Status of Married Women in Lebanon." *International Journal of Middle East Studies* 30, no. 4 (Nov. 1998): 501–19.

Singh, Alka. *Women in Muslim Personal Law*. Jaipur, India: Rawat Publications, 1992.

Smith, Jane I., ed. *Women in Contemporary Muslim Societies*. Lewisburg, Pa.: Bucknell Univ. Press, 1980.

———. "Women, Religion and Social Change in Early Islam." In *Women, Religion and Social Change*. Edited by Yvonne Yazbeck Haddad and Ellison Banks Findley. Syracuse: Syracuse Univ. Press, 1985, 19–35.

Smith, W. Robertson. *Kinship and Marriage in Early Arabia*. Boston: Beacon Press, 1903.

Stern, Gertrude. *Marriage in Early Islam*. London: Routledge and Kegan Paul, 1939.

Tadros, Mariz. "One Step Forward, A Hundred To Go,' *Al-Ahram Weekly*. 464 (January 2000): 13–19.

Tyabji, Faiz Badruddin. *Muhammadan Law: The Personal Law of Muslims*. 3rd ed. Bombay: N. M. Tripathi, 1940.

Tyan, E. *Histoire de l'organisation judiciaire en Pays d'Islam*. 2d ed. Leiden: Brill, 1960.

Vesey-Fitzgerald, Seymour. *Muhammadan Law: An Abridgement*. London: Oxford Univ. Press, 1931.

von Grunebaum, G. E. *Medieval Islam*. Chicago: Univ. of Chicago Press, 1947.

Wadud, Amina. *Quran and Woman: Rereading the Sacred Text from a Woman's Perspective*. 2d ed. New York: Oxford Univ. Press, 1999.

Woodsmall, Ruth F. *Women and the New East*. Washington, D.C.: Middle East Institute, 1960.

Index

Index

Index

Index